CONTEN

Column 1
The date

Column 3 (Common Worship)
On Principal Feasts, Principal Holy Days, Sundays and Festivals this gives the Principal Service Lectionary, intended for use at the main service of the day (in most churches the mid-morning service), whether or not it is a Eucharist.

On other weekdays this gives the Daily Eucharistic Lectionary for those wanting a semi-continuous pattern of readings and a psalm for Holy Communion. It is most useful in a church where there is a daily celebration and a core community that worships together day by day, though its use is not restricted to that.

Column 4 (Common Worship)
On Principal Feasts, Principal Holy Days, Sundays and Festivals this gives the Third Service Lectionary. Many churches will have no need of it, for it comes into use only if the Principal and Second Service Lectionaries have been used. Its most likely use is at Morning Prayer (when this is not the Principal Service). Where psalms are recommended for use in the morning, these also appear in this column.

On other weekdays this provides the psalmody and readings for Morning Prayer. Where two or more psalms are appointed, the psalm in bold italic may be used as the only psalm. Psalms printed in round brackets ( ) may be omitted if they are used as an opening canticle at Morning Prayer. Where † is printed after the psalm number, the psalm may be shortened if desired. For those wishing to follow the Ordinary Time psalm cycle throughout the year (except for the period between 19 December and the Epiphany and from the Monday of Holy Week to the Saturday of Easter Week), this is printed as an alternative to the seasonal provision.

COMMON WORSHIP

July 2017

		COMMON WORSHIP	Sunday Principal Service Weekday Eucharist	Third Service Morning Prayer
22	Sa	MARY MAGDALENE	Song of Sol. 3. 1–4 Ps. 42. 1–10 2 Cor. 5. 14–17 John 20. 1–2, 11–18	MP: Ps. 30; 32; 150 1 Sam. 16. 14–end Luke 8. 1–3
	W			
23	S	THE SIXTH SUNDAY AFTER TRINITY **(Proper 11)**		
		Track 1 Gen. 28. 10–19a Ps. 139. 1–11, 23–24 (or 139. 1–11) Rom. 8. 12–25 Matt. 13. 24–30, 36–43	*Track 2* Wisd. 12. 13, 16–19 or Isa. 44. 6–8 Ps. 86. 11–end Rom. 8. 12–25 Matt. 13. 24–30, 36–43	Ps. 71 Deut. 30. 1–10 1 Pet. 3. 8–18
	G			
24 DEL 16	M		Exod. 14. 5–18 Ps. 136. 1–4, 10–15 or *Canticle*: Exod. 15. 1–6 Matt. 12. 38–42	Ps. 123; 124; 125; *126* Ezek. 10. 1–19 2 Cor. 6.1 – 7.1
	G			

Column 2 provides for Common Worship:
  * the name of the Principal Holy Day, Sunday, Festival or Lesser Festival;
  * a note of other Commemorations for mention in prayers;
  * any general note that applies to the whole *Common Worship* provision for the day;
  * one of the options where there are two options for readings at the Eucharist or Principal Service;
  * an indication of the liturgical colour.

Readings: Readings occur in this column only in two circumstances. On Sundays after Trinity where there are two 'tracks' for the Principal Service readings (where there is a choice of first reading and psalm, but the second reading and Gospel are the same in both tracks), Track 1 appears in this column. On Lesser Festivals throughout the year, where there are readings for that festival that are alternative to the semi-continuous Daily Eucharistic Lectionary, these also appear in this column.

Colour: An upper-case letter indicates the liturgical colour of the day. A lower-case second colour indicates the colour for a Lesser Festival while the upper-case letter indicates the continuing seasonal colour.

Week number of Daily Eucharistic Lectionary

LECTIONARY

Column 5 (Common Worship)
On Principal Feasts, Principal Holy Days, Sundays and Festivals this gives the Second Service Lectionary, intended for use when a second set of readings is required. Its most likely use is in the evening, when the Principal Service Lectionary has been used in the morning. Sometimes it might be used at an evening Eucharist. Where the second reading is not a Gospel reading, an alternative to meet this need is provided. Where psalms are recommended for use in the evening, these also appear in this column.

On other weekdays this provides the psalmody and readings for Evening Prayer. Where two or more psalms are provided, the psalm in bold italic may be used as the only psalm. Psalms printed in round brackets ( ) may be omitted if they are used as an opening canticle at Evening Prayer. Where † is printed after the psalm number, the psalm may be shortened if desired. For those wishing to follow the Ordinary Time psalm cycle throughout the year (except for the period between 19 December and the Epiphany and from the Monday of Holy Week to the Saturday of Easter Week), this is printed as an alternative to the seasonal provision.

Column 7 (Book of Common Prayer)
This provides the readings for Morning Prayer, together with psalm provision where it varies from the BCP monthly cycle.

A letter to indicate liturgical colour in this column indicates a change of colour before Evening Prayer. The symbol in bold lower case, **ct**, indicates that the Collect at Evening Prayer should be that of the following day.

BOOK OF COMMON PRAYER

Second Service Evening Prayer		Calendar and Holy Communion	Morning Prayer	Evening Prayer
		MARY MAGDALENE		
EP: Ps. 63		Zeph. 3. 14–end	(Ps. 30; 32; 150)	(Ps. 63)
Zeph. 3. 14–end		Ps. 30. 1–5	I Sam. 16. 14–end	Song of Sol. 3. 1–4
Mark 15.40 – 16.7		2 Cor. 5. 14–17	Luke 8. 1–3	Mark 15.40 – 16.7
	W	John 20. 11–18		
		THE SIXTH SUNDAY AFTER TRINITY		
Ps. 67; [70]		Gen. 4. 2b–15	Ps. 71	Ps. 67; [70]
I Kings 2. 10–12; 3. 16–end		Ps. 90. 12–end	Deut. 30. 1–10	I Kings 2. 10–12;
Acts 4. 1–22		Rom. 6. 3–11	I Pet. 3. 13–22	3. 16–end
Gospel: Mark 6. 30–34, 53–end		Matt. 5. 20–26		Acts 4. 1–22
	G			
Ps. *127*; 128; 129			Ezek. 10. 1–19	I Sam. ch. 5
I Sam. ch. 5			2 Cor. 6.1 – 7.1	Luke 20.41 – 21.4
Luke 20.41 – 21.4				or First EP of James
or First EP of James				(Ps. 144)
Ps. 144				Deut. 30. 11–end
Deut. 30. 11–end				Mark 5. 21–end
Mark 5. 21–end				
R ct	G			R ct

A letter to indicate liturgical colour in this column indicates a change of colour before Evening Prayer. The symbol in bold lower case, **ct**, indicates that the Collect at Evening Prayer should be that of the following day.

Column 6 provides for Book of Common Prayer:
• the name of the Principal Holy Day, Sunday, Festival or Lesser Festival;
• any general note that applies to the whole Prayer Book provision for the day and an indication of points at which users may wish to draw on *Common Worship* material on the opposite page where the BCP has no provision;
• the Lectionary for the Eucharist on any day for which provision is made;
• an indication of liturgical colour (see column 2).

Column 8 (Book of Common Prayer)
This provides the readings for Evening Prayer, together with psalm provision where it varies from the BCP monthly cycle.

Making Choices in *Common Worship*

Common Worship makes provision for a variety of pastoral and liturgical circumstances. It needs to, for it has to serve some church communities where Morning Prayer, Holy Communion and Evening Prayer are all celebrated every day, and yet be useful also in a church with only one service a week, and that service varying in form and time from week to week.

At the beginning of the year, some decisions in principle need to be taken.

In relation to the Calendar, a decision needs to be taken whether to keep The Epiphany on Friday 6 January or on Sunday 8 January, whether to keep The Presentation of Christ (Candlemas) on Thursday 2 February or on Sunday 29 January, and whether to keep the Feast of All Saints on Wednesday 1 November or on Sunday 5 November.

In relation to the Lectionary, the initial choices every year to decide in relation to Sundays are:

- which of the services on a Principal Feast, Principal Holy Day, Sunday or Festival constitutes the 'Principal Service'; then use the Principal Service Lectionary (column 3) consistently for that service through the year;
- during the Sundays after Trinity, whether to use Track I of the Principal Service Lectionary (column 2), where the first reading stays over several weeks with one Old Testament book read semi-continuously, or Track 2 (column 3), where the first reading is chosen for its relationship to the Gospel reading of the day;
- which, if any, service on a Principal Feast, Principal Holy Day, Sunday or Festival constitutes the 'Second Service'; then use the Second Service Lectionary (column 5) consistently for that service through the year;
- which, if any, service on a Principal Feast, Principal Holy Day, Sunday or Festival constitutes the 'Third Service'; then use the Third Service Lectionary (column 4) consistently for that service through the year.

And in relation to weekdays:

- whether to use the Daily Eucharistic Lectionary (column 3) consistently for weekday celebrations of Holy Communion (with the exception of Principal Feasts, Principal Holy Days and Festivals) or to make some use of the Lesser Festival provision;
- whether to follow the first psalm provision in column 4 (morning) and column 5 (evening), where psalms during the seasons have a seasonal flavour but in ordinary time follow a sequential pattern; or to follow the alternative provision in the same columns, where psalms follow the sequential pattern throughout the year, except for the period between 19 December and The Epiphany and from the Monday of Holy Week to the Saturday of Easter Week; or to follow the psalm cycle in the Book of Common Prayer, where they are nearly always used 'in course';
- whether to use the Additional Weekday Lectionary (which begins on page 92) for weekday services (other than Holy Communion). It provides a one-year cycle of two readings for each day (except for Sundays, Principal Feasts, Principal Holy Days, Festivals and during Holy Week). Since each of the readings is designed to 'stand alone' (that is, it is complete in itself and will make sense to the worshipper who has not attended on the previous day and who will not be present on the next day), it is intended particularly for use in those churches and cathedrals that attract occasional rather than regular congregations.

The flexibility of *Common Worship* is intended to enable the church and the minister to find the most helpful provision for them. But once a decision is made, it is advisable to stay with that decision through the year or at the very least through a complete season.

All Bible references (except to the psalms) are to the New Revised Standard Version, Anglicized edition (1995). Those who use other Bible translations should check the verse numbers against the NRSV. References to the psalms are to the *Common Worship* Psalter.

Book of Common Prayer

A separate Lectionary for the Book of Common Prayer is no longer issued. Provision is made on the right-hand pages of this Lectionary for BCP worship on all Sundays in the year, for the major festivals and for Morning and Evening Prayer. The Epistles and Gospels for Holy Communion are those of 1662, with the additions and variations of 1928, now authorized under the *Common Worship* overall provision. The Old Testament readings and psalms for these services, formerly appended to the Series One Holy Communion service, may be used but are not mandatory with the 1662 order.

Readings for Morning and Evening Prayer, which are the same as those for *Common Worship*, are set out in the BCP section for Sundays and weekdays. The special psalm provision of the BCP is given; however, where the *Common Worship* psalm provision is used, verse numbering may occasionally differ slightly from that in the BCP Psalter, and appropriate adjustment will have to be made (a table of variations in verse numbering can be found at www.churchofengland.org/prayer-worship/worship/texts/daily2/psalter/psalterverses.aspx). Otherwise the Psalter is read in course daily through each month.

The Calendar observes BCP dates when these differ from those of *Common Worship*; for example, St Thomas on 21 December. Additional commemorations in the *Common Worship* Calendar are not included, but those who wish to observe them may use the *Collects and Post Communions in Traditional Language: Lesser Festivals, Common of the Saints, Special Occasions* (Church House Publishing).

The Lectionaries of 1871 and 1922, to be found in many copies of the BCP, are still authorized and may be used, but – with the exception of the psalms and readings for Holy Communion mentioned above – the Additional Alternative Lectionary (1961) is no longer authorized for public worship.

Although those who use the BCP, for private or public worship or both, are free to follow any of the authorized lectionaries, there is much to be said for common usage across the Church of England, so that the same passages are being read by all. It is of course appropriate that BCP readings should be taken from the Authorized or King James Version for harmony of style, with the daily recitation of the BCP Psalter.

The integrity of the BCP as the traditional source of worship in the Church of England is not in any way affected by the use of a common lectionary for the daily offices.

CERTAIN DAYS AND OCCASIONS COMMONLY OBSERVED

Plough Sunday may be observed on 8 January 2017.

The Week of Prayer for Christian Unity may be observed from 18 to 25 January 2017.

Education Sunday may be observed on 12 February 2017.

Rogation Sunday may be observed on 21 May 2017.

The Feast of Dedication is observed on the anniversary of the dedication or consecration of a church, or, when the actual date is unknown, on 1 October 2017. In CW, 29 October 2017 is an alternative date.

Ember Days. CW encourages the bishop to set the Ember Days in each diocese in the week before the ordinations, whereas in BCP the dates are fixed.

Days of Discipline and Self-Denial in CW are the weekdays of Lent and all Fridays in the year, except all Principal Feasts and festivals outside Lent and Fridays between Easter Day and Pentecost. The eves of Principal Feasts are also appropriately kept as days of discipline and self-denial in preparation for the feast.

Days of Fasting and Abstinence according to the BCP are the forty days of Lent, the Ember Days at the four seasons, the three Rogation Days, and all Fridays in the year except Christmas Day. The BCP also orders the observance of the Evens or Vigils before The Nativity of our Lord, The Purification of the Blessed Virgin Mary, The Annunciation of the Blessed Virgin Mary, Easter Day, Ascension Day, Pentecost, and before the following saints' days: Matthias, John the Baptist, Peter, James, Bartholomew, Matthew, Simon and Jude, Andrew, Thomas, and All Saints. (If any of these days falls on Monday, the Vigil is to be kept on the previous Saturday.)

KEY TO LITURGICAL COLOURS

Common Worship suggests appropriate liturgical colours. They are not mandatory, and traditional or local use may be followed.

For a detailed discussion of when colours may be used, see *Common Worship: Services and Prayers for the Church of England* (Church House Publishing), *New Handbook of Pastoral Liturgy* (SPCK) or *A Companion to Common Worship: Volume I* (SPCK).

W White
ꟿ Gold or white
R Red
P Purple (may vary from 'Roman purple' to violet, with blue as an alternative; a Lent array of sackcloth may be used in Lent, and rose pink on The Third Sunday of Advent and Fourth Sunday of Lent)
G Green

When a lower-case letter accompanies an upper-case letter, the lower-case letter indicates the liturgical colour appropriate to the Lesser Festival of that day, while the upper-case letter indicates the continuing seasonal colour.

PRINCIPAL FEASTS, HOLY DAYS AND FESTIVALS

Principal Feasts, and other Principal Holy Days (Ash Wednesday, Maundy Thursday, Good Friday) are printed in **LARGE BOLD CAPITALS** in the Lectionary.

There are no longer proper readings relating to the Holy Spirit on the six days after Pentecost. Instead they have been located on the nine days before Pentecost.

When Patronal and Dedication Festivals are kept as Principal Feasts, they may be transferred to the nearest Sunday, unless that day is already either a Principal Feast or The First Sunday of Advent, The Baptism of Christ, The First Sunday of Lent or Palm Sunday.

Festivals are printed in the Lectionary in SMALL BOLD CAPITALS.

For each day there is a full liturgical provision for the Holy Communion and for Morning and Evening Prayer. Most holy days that are in the category 'Festival' are provided with an optional First Evening Prayer. Its use is entirely at the discretion of the minister. Where it is used, the liturgical colour for the next day should be used at that First Evening Prayer, and this has been indicated in the provision on the following pages.

LESSER FESTIVALS AND COMMEMORATIONS

Lesser Festivals (printed in **bold roman** typeface) are observed at the level appropriate to a particular church. The readings and psalms for The Common of the Saints are listed on page 9. In addition, there are special readings appropriate to the Festival listed in the first column. The daily psalms and readings at Morning and Evening Prayer are not usually superseded by those for Lesser Festivals, but the readings and psalms for Holy Communion may on occasion be used at Morning or Evening Prayer.

Commemorations are printed in the Lectionary in *italic* typeface. They do not have collect, psalm or readings, but may be observed by mention in prayers of intercession and thanksgiving. For local reasons, or where there is an established tradition in the wider Church, they may be kept as Lesser Festivals using the appropriate material from The Common of the Saints. Equally, it may be desirable to observe some Lesser Festivals as Commemorations.

If a Lesser Festival or a Commemoration falls on a Principal Feast, Principal Holy Day, Sunday or Festival, it is not normally observed that year, although it may be celebrated, where there is sufficient reason, on the nearest available day. Lesser Festivals and Commemorations which, for this reason, would not be celebrated in 2016–17 are listed on pages 7–8, so that, if desired, they may be mentioned in prayers of intercession and thanksgiving.

LESSER FESTIVALS AND COMMEMORATIONS NOT OBSERVED IN 2016–17

The Lesser Festivals and Commemorations (shown in italics) listed below fall on a Sunday or during Holy Week or Easter Week this year, and are thus not observed in this Lectionary.

Common Worship

2016

December

4   *John of Damascus, Monk, Teacher, c. 749*
     Nicholas Ferrar, Deacon, Founder of the Little Gidding Community, 1637

2017

January

22   *Vincent of Saragossa, Deacon, first Martyr of Spain, 304*

March

1   David, Bishop of Menevia, Patron of Wales, c. 601
20   Cuthbert, Bishop of Lindisfarne, Missionary, 687
26   *Harriet Monsell, Founder of the Community of St John the Baptist, Clewer, 1883*

April

9   *Dietrich Bonhoeffer, Lutheran Pastor, Martyr, 1945*
10   William Law, Priest, Spiritual Writer, 1761
     William of Ockham, Friar, Philosopher, Teacher, 1347
11   *George Augustus Selwyn, first Bishop of New Zealand, 1878*
16   *Isabella Gilmore, Deaconess, 1923*
19   Alphege, Archbishop of Canterbury, Martyr, 1012
21   Anselm, Abbot of Le Bec, Archbishop of Canterbury, Teacher, 1109
24   *Mellitus, Bishop of London, first Bishop at St Paul's, 624*
     The Seven Martyrs of the Melanesian Brotherhood, Solomon Islands, 2003
30   *Pandita Mary Ramabai, Translator of the Scriptures, 1922*

May

21   *Helena, Protector of the Holy Places, 330*
25   The Venerable Bede, Monk at Jarrow, Scholar, Historian, 735
     Aldhelm, Bishop of Sherborne, 709
28   *Lanfranc, Prior of Le Bec, Archbishop of Canterbury, Scholar, 1089*

June

4   *Petroc, Abbot of Padstow, 6th century*
18   *Bernard Mizeki, Apostle of the MaShona, Martyr, 1896*

July

16   *Osmund, Bishop of Salisbury, 1099*
23   *Bridget of Sweden, Abbess of Vadstena, 1373*
30   William Wilberforce, Social Reformer, Olaudah Equiano and Thomas Clarkson, Anti-Slavery Campaigners, 1833, 1797 and 1846

August

13   Jeremy Taylor, Bishop of Down and Connor, Teacher, 1667
     Florence Nightingale, Nurse, Social Reformer, 1910
     Octavia Hill, Social Reformer, 1912

20	Bernard, Abbot of Clairvaux, Teacher, 1153
	William and Catherine Booth, Founders of the Salvation Army, 1912 and 1890
27	Monica, Mother of Augustine of Hippo, 387

September

| 3 | Gregory the Great, Bishop of Rome, Teacher, 604 |
| 17 | Hildegard, Abbess of Bingen, Visionary, 1179 |

October

1	*Remigius, Bishop of Rheims, Apostle of the Franks, 533*
	Anthony Ashley Cooper, Earl of Shaftesbury, Social Reformer, 1885
15	Teresa of Avila, Teacher, 1582
29	James Hannington, Bishop of Eastern Equatorial Africa, Martyr in Uganda, 1885

November

| 19 | Hilda, Abbess of Whitby, 680 |
| | *Mechtild, Béguine of Magdeburg, Mystic, 1280* |

December

3	*Francis Xavier, Missionary, Apostle of the Indies, 1552*
17	*Eglantyne Jebb, Social Reformer, Founder of Save the Children, 1928*
31	*John Wyclif, Reformer, 1384*

Book of Common Prayer

2017

January

| 8 | Lucian, Priest and Martyr, 290 |
| 22 | Vincent of Saragossa, Deacon, first Martyr of Spain, 304 |

February

| 5 | Agatha, Martyr in Sicily, 251 |

March

| 1 | David, Bishop of Menevia, Patron of Wales, c. 601 |
| 12 | Gregory the Great, Bishop of Rome, 604 |

April

| 19 | Alphege, Archbishop of Canterbury, Martyr, 1012 |

June

| 5 | Boniface (Wynfrith) of Crediton, Bishop, Apostle of Germany, Martyr, 754 |

July

| 2 | The Visitation of the Blessed Virgin Mary |

September

| 17 | Lambert, Bishop of Maastricht, Martyr, 709 |

October

| 1 | Remigius, Bishop of Rheims, Apostle of the Franks, 533 |

December

| 31 | Silvester, Bishop of Rome, 335 |

THE COMMON OF THE SAINTS

The Blessed Virgin Mary

Genesis 3. 8–15, 20; Isaiah 7. 10–14; Micah 5. 1–4

Psalms 45. 10–17; 113; 131

Acts 1. 12–14; Romans 8. 18–30; Galatians 4. 4–7

Luke 1. 26–38; Luke 1. 39–47; John 19. 25–27

Martyrs

2 Chronicles 24. 17–21; Isaiah 43. 1–7; Jeremiah 11. 18–20; Wisdom 4. 10–15

Psalms 3; 11; 31. 1–5; 44. 18–24; 126

Romans 8. 35–end; 2 Corinthians 4. 7–15; 2 Timothy 2. 3–7 [8–13]; Hebrews 11. 32–end; 1 Peter 4. 12–end; Revelation 12. 10–12a

Matthew 10. 16–22; Matthew 10. 28–39; Matthew 16. 24–26; John 12. 24–26; John 15. 18–21

Teachers of the Faith and Spiritual Writers

1 Kings 3. [6–10] 11–14; Proverbs 4. 1–9; Wisdom 7. 7–10, 15–16; Ecclesiasticus 39. 1–10

Psalms 19. 7–10; 34. 11–17; 37. 31–35; 119. 89–96; 119. 97–104

1 Corinthians 1. 18–25; 1 Corinthians 2. 1–10; 1 Corinthians 2. 9–end;

Ephesians 3. 8–12; 2 Timothy 4. 1–8; Titus 2. 1–8

Matthew 5. 13–19; Matthew 13. 52–end; Matthew 23. 8–12; Mark 4. 1–9; John 16. 12–15

Bishops and Other Pastors

1 Samuel 16. 1, 6–13; Isaiah 6. 1–8; Jeremiah 1. 4–10; Ezekiel 3. 16–21; Malachi 2. 5–7

Psalms 1; 15; 16. 5–end; 96; 110

Acts 20. 28–35; 1 Corinthians 4. 1–5; 2 Corinthians 4. 1–10 (or 1–2, 5–7); 2 Corinthians 5. 14–20; 1 Peter 5. 1–4

Matthew 11. 25–end; Matthew 24. 42–46; John 10. 11–16; John 15. 9–17; John 21. 15–17

Members of Religious Communities

1 Kings 19. 9–18; Proverbs 10. 27–end; Song of Solomon 8. 6–7; Isaiah 61.10 – 62.5; Hosea 2. 14–15, 19–20

Psalms 34. 1–8; 112. 1–9; 119. 57–64; 123; 131

Acts 4. 32–35; 2 Corinthians 10.17 – 11.2; Philippians 3. 7–14; 1 John 2. 15–17; Revelation 19. 1, 5–9

Matthew 11. 25–end; Matthew 19. 3–12; Matthew 19. 23–end; Luke 9. 57–end; Luke 12. 32–37

Missionaries

Isaiah 52. 7–10; Isaiah 61. 1–3a; Ezekiel 34. 11–16; Jonah 3. 1–5

Psalms 67; 87; 97; 100; 117

Acts 2. 14, 22–36; Acts 13. 46–49; Acts 16. 6–10; Acts 26. 19–23; Romans 15. 17–21; 2 Corinthians 5.11 – 6.2

Matthew 9. 35–end; Matthew 28. 16–end; Mark 16. 15–20; Luke 5. 1–11; Luke 10. 1–9

Any Saint

Genesis 12. 1–4; Proverbs 8. 1–11; Micah 6. 6–8; Ecclesiasticus 2. 7–13 [14–end]

Psalms 32; 33. 1–5; 119. 1–8; 139. 1–4 [5–12]; 145. 8–14

Ephesians 3. 14–19; Ephesians 6. 11–18; Hebrews 13. 7–8, 15–16; James 2. 14–17; 1 John 4. 7–16; Revelation 21. [1–4] 5–7

Matthew 19. 16–21; Matthew 25. 1–13; Matthew 25. 14–30; John 15. 1–8; John 17. 20–end

---

SPECIAL OCCASIONS

The Guidance of the Holy Spirit
Proverbs 24. 3–7; Isaiah 30. 15–21; Wisdom 9. 13–17
Psalms 25. 1–9; 104. 26–33; 143. 8–10
Acts 15. 23–29; Romans 8. 22–27; 1 Corinthians 12. 4–13
Luke 14. 27–33; John 14. 23–26; John 16. 13–15

The Commemoration of the Faithful Departed
Lamentations 3. 17–26, 31–33 or Wisdom 3. 1–9
Psalm 23 or Psalm 27. 1–6, 16–end
Romans 5. 5–11 or 1 Peter 1. 3–9
John 5. 19–25 or John 6. 37–40

Rogation Days
Deuteronomy 8. 1–10; 1 Kings 8. 35–40; Job 28. 1–11
Psalms 104. 21–30; 107. 1–9; 121
Philippians 4. 4–7; 2 Thessalonians 3. 6–13; 1 John 5. 12–15
Matthew 6. 1–15; Mark 11. 22–24; Luke 11. 5–13

Harvest Thanksgiving
Year A
Deuteronomy 8. 7–18 or Deuteronomy 28. 1–14
Psalm 65
2 Corinthians 9. 6–end
Luke 12. 16–30 or Luke 17. 11–19

Year B
Joel 2. 21–27
Psalm 126
1 Timothy 2. 1–7 or 1 Timothy 6. 6–10
Matthew 6. 25–33

Year C
Deuteronomy 26. 1–11
Psalm 100
Philippians 4. 4–9 or Revelation 14. 14–18
John 6. 25–35

Mission and Evangelism
Isaiah 49. 1–6; Isaiah 52. 7–10; Micah 4. 1–5
Psalms 2; 46; 67
Acts 17. 12–end; 2 Corinthians 5.14 – 6.2; Ephesians 2. 13–end
Matthew 5. 13–16; Matthew 28. 16–end; John 17. 20–end

The Unity of the Church
Jeremiah 33. 6–9a; Ezekiel 36. 23–28; Zephaniah 3. 16–end
Psalms 100; 122; 133
Ephesians 4. 1–6; Colossians 3. 9–17; 1 John 4. 9–15
Matthew 18. 19–22; John 11. 45–52; John 17. 11b–23

The Peace of the World

Isaiah 9. 1–6; Isaiah 57. 15–19; Micah 4. 1–5
Psalms 40. 14–17; 72. 1–7; 85. 8–13
Philippians 4. 6–9; 1 Timothy 2. 1–6; James 3. 13–18
Matthew 5. 43–end; John 14. 23–29; John 15. 9–17

Social Justice and Responsibility

Isaiah 32. 15–end; Amos 5. 21–24; Amos 8. 4–7; Acts 5. 1–11
Psalms 31. 21–24; 85. 1–7; 146. 5–10
Colossians 3. 12–15; James 2. 1–4
Matthew 5. 1–12; Matthew 25. 31–end; Luke 16. 19–end

Ministry (including Ember Days)

Numbers 11. 16–17, 24–29; Numbers 27. 15–end; 1 Samuel 16. 1–13a
Isaiah 6. 1–8; Isaiah 61. 1–3; Jeremiah 1. 4–10
Psalms 40. 8–13; 84. 8–12; 89. 19–25; 101. 1–5, 7; 122
Acts 20. 28–35; 1 Corinthians 3. 3–11; Ephesians 4. 4–16; Philippians 3. 7–14
Luke 4. 16–21; Luke 12. 35–43; Luke 22. 24–27; John 4. 31–38; John 15. 5–17

In Time of Trouble

Genesis 9. 8–17; Job 1. 13–end; Isaiah 38. 6–11
Psalms 86. 1–7; 107. 4–15; 142. 1–7
Romans 3. 21–26; Romans 8. 18–25; 2 Corinthians 8. 1–5, 9
Mark 4. 35–end; Luke 12. 1–7; John 16. 31–end

For the Sovereign

Joshua 1. 1–9; Proverbs 8. 1–16
Psalms 20; 101; 121
Romans 13. 1–10; Revelation 21.22 – 22.4
Matthew 22. 16–22; Luke 22. 24–30

November 2016

			Sunday Principal Service Weekday Eucharist	Third Service Morning Prayer
27	S	THE FIRST SUNDAY OF ADVENT CW Year A begins		
			Isa. 2. 1–5 Ps. 122 Rom. 13. 11–end	Ps. 44 Micah 4. 1–7 1 Thess. 5. 1–11
	P		Matt. 24. 36–44	
28	M	Daily Eucharistic Lectionary Year 1 begins		
			Isa. 4. 2–end Ps. 122 Matt. 8. 5–11	Ps. *50*; 54 *alt.* Ps. *1*; 2; 3 Isa. 42. 18–end
	P			Rev. ch. 19
29	Tu		Isa. 11. 1–10 Ps. 72. 1–4, 18–19 Luke 10. 21–24	Ps. *80*; 82 *alt.* Ps. *5*; 6; (8) Isa. 43. 1–13 Rev. ch. 20
		Day of Intercession and Thanksgiving for the Missionary Work of the Church Isa. 49. 1–6; Isa. 52. 7–10; Mic. 4. 1–5 Acts 17. 12–end; 2 Cor. 5.14 – 6.2; Eph. 2. 13–end Ps. 2; 46; 47		
	P	Matt. 5. 13–16; Matt. 28. 16–end; John 17. 20–end		
30	W	ANDREW THE APOSTLE		
			Isa. 52. 7–10 Ps. 19. 1–6 Rom. 10. 12–18	*MP:* Ps. 47; 147. 1–12 Ezek. 47. 1–12 *or* Ecclus. 14. 20–end
	R		Matt. 4. 18–22	John 12. 20–32

December 2016

1	Th	*Charles de Foucauld, Hermit in the Sahara, 1916*		
			Isa. 26. 1–6 Ps. 118. 18–27a Matt. 7. 21, 24–27	Ps. *42*; 43 *alt.* Ps. 14; *15*; 16 Isa. 44. 1–8
	P			Rev. 21. 9–21
2	F		Isa. 29. 17–end Ps. 27. 1–4, 16–17 Matt. 9. 27–31	Ps. *25*; 26 *alt.* Ps. 17; *19* Isa. 44. 9–23
	P			Rev. 21.22 – 22.5
3	Sa	*Francis Xavier, Missionary, Apostle of the Indies, 1552*		
			Isa. 30. 19–21, 23–26 Ps. 146. 4–9 Matt. 9.35 – 10.1, 6–8	Ps. *9*; (10) *alt.* Ps. 20; 21; *23* Isa. 44.24 – 45.13
	P			Rev. 22. 6–end
4	S	THE SECOND SUNDAY OF ADVENT		
			Isa. 11. 1–10 Ps. 72. 1–7, 18–19 (*or* 72. 1–7) Rom. 15. 4–13	Ps. 80 Amos ch. 7 Luke 1. 5–20
	P		Matt. 3. 1–12	
5	M		Isa. ch. 35 Ps. 85. 7–end Luke 5. 17–26	Ps. 44 *alt.* Ps. 27; *30* Isa. 45. 14–end
	P			1 Thess. ch. 1

Second Service Evening Prayer		Calendar and Holy Communion	Morning Prayer	Evening Prayer
Ps. 9 (or 9. 1–8) Isa. 52. 1–12 Matt. 24. 15–28		**THE FIRST SUNDAY IN ADVENT** Advent I Collect until Christmas Eve Mic. 4. 1–4, 6–7 Ps. 25. 1–9 Rom. 13. 8–14 **P** Matt. 21. 1–13	Ps. 44 Isa. 2. 1–5 I Thess. 5. 1–11	Ps. 9 (or 9. 1–8) Isa. 52. 1–12 Matt. 24. 15–28
Ps. 70; *71* *alt.* Ps. *4*; 7 Isa. 25. 1–9 Matt. 12. 1–21		**P**	Isa. 42. 18–end Rev. ch. 19	Isa. 25. 1–9 Matt. 12. 1–21
Ps. *74*; 75 *alt.* Ps. *9*; 10† Isa. 26. 1–13 Matt. 12. 22–37 *or First EP of Andrew the Apostle* Ps. 48 Isa. 49. 1–9a I Cor. 4. 9–16			Isa. 43. 1–13 Rev. ch. 20	Isa. 26. 1–13 Matt. 12. 22–37 *or First EP of Andrew the Apostle* (Ps. 48) Isa. 49. 1–9a I Cor. 4. 9–16
		To celebrate the Day of Intercession and Thanksgiving for the Missionary Work of the Church, see *Common Worship* provision.		
R ct	**P**			**R ct**
EP: Ps. 87; 96 Zech. 8. 20–end John 1. 35–42		**ANDREW THE APOSTLE** Zech. 8. 20–end Ps. 92. 1–5 Rom. 10. 9–end **R** Matt. 4. 18–22	(Ps. 47; 147. 1–12) Ezek. 47. 1–12 *or* Ecclus. 14. 20–end John 12. 20–32	(Ps. 87; 96) Isa. 52. 7–10 John 1. 35–42
Ps. *40*; 46 *alt.* Ps. 18† Isa. 28. 14–end Matt. 13. 1–23		**P**	Isa. 44. 1–8 Rev. 21. 9–21	Isa. 28. 14–end Matt. 13. 1–23
Ps. 16; *17* *alt.* Ps. 22 Isa. 29. 1–14 Matt. 13. 24–43		**P**	Isa. 44. 9–23 Rev. 21.22 – 22.5	Isa. 29. 1–14 Matt. 13. 24–43
Ps. *27*; 28 *alt.* Ps. *24*; 25 Isa. 29. 15–end Matt. 13. 44–end ct		**P**	Isa. 44.24 – 45.13 Rev. 22. 6–end	Isa. 29. 15–end Matt. 13. 44–end ct
Ps. 11; [28] I Kings 18. 17–39 John 1. 19–28		**THE SECOND SUNDAY IN ADVENT** 2 Kings 22. 8–10; 23. 1–3 Ps. 50. 1–6 Rom. 15. 4–13 **P** Luke 21. 25–33	Ps. 80 Amos ch. 7 Luke 1. 5–20	Ps. 11; [28] I Kings 18. 17–39 Matt. 3. 1–12
Ps. *144*; 146 *alt.* Ps. 26; *28*; 29 Isa. 30. 1–18 Matt. 14. 1–12		**P**	Isa. 45. 14–end I Thess. ch. 1	Isa. 30. 1–18 Matt. 14. 1–12

December 2016

			Sunday Principal Service / Weekday Eucharist	Third Service / Morning Prayer
6	Tu	**Nicholas, Bishop of Myra, c. 326** Com. Bishop *also* Isa. 61. 1–3 1 Tim. 6. 6–11	*or* Isa. 40. 1–11 Ps. 96. 1, 10–end Matt. 18. 12–14	Ps. *56*; 57 *alt.* Ps. 32; *36* Isa. ch. 46
	Pw	Mark 10. 13–16		1 Thess. 2. 1–12
7	W	**Ambrose, Bishop of Milan, Teacher, 397** Ember Day* Com. Teacher *also* Isa. 41. 9b–13 Luke 22. 24–30	*or* Isa. 40. 25–end Ps. 103. 8–13 Matt. 11. 28–end	Ps. *62*; 63 *alt.* Ps. 34 Isa. ch. 47
	Pw			1 Thess. 2. 13–end
8	Th	**The Conception of the Blessed Virgin Mary** Com. BVM	*or* Isa. 41. 13–20 Ps. 145. 1, 8–13 Matt. 11. 11–15	Ps. 53; *54*; 60 *alt.* Ps. 37† Isa. 48. 1–11
	Pw			1 Thess. ch. 3
9	F	Ember Day*	Isa. 48. 17–19 Ps. 1 Matt. 11. 16–19	Ps. 85; *86* *alt.* Ps. 31 Isa. 48. 12–end
	P			1 Thess. 4. 1–12
10	Sa	Ember Day*	Ecclus. 48. 1–4, 9–11 *or* 2 Kings 2. 9–12 Ps. 80. 1–4, 18–19 Matt. 17. 10–13	Ps. 145 *alt.* Ps. 41; *42*; 43 Isa. 49. 1–13
	P			1 Thess. 4. 13–end
11	S	THE THIRD SUNDAY OF ADVENT	Isa. 35. 1–10 Ps. 146. 4–10 *or Canticle*: Magnificat James 5. 7–10	Ps. 68. 1–19 Zeph. 3. 14–end Phil. 4. 4–7
	P		Matt. 11. 2–11	
12	M		Num. 24. 2–7, 15–17 Ps. 25. 3–8 Matt. 21. 23–27	Ps. 40 *alt.* Ps. 44 Isa. 49. 14–25
	P			1 Thess. 5. 1–11
13	Tu	**Lucy, Martyr at Syracuse, 304** *Samuel Johnson, Moralist, 1784* Com. Martyr *also* Wisd. 3. 1–7 2 Cor. 4. 6–15	*or* Zeph. 3. 1–2, 9–13 Ps. 34. 1–6, 21–22 Matt. 21. 28–32	Ps. *70*; 74 *alt.* Ps. *48*; 52 Isa. ch. 50
	Pr			1 Thess. 5. 12–end
14	W	**John of the Cross, Poet, Teacher, 1591** Com. Teacher *esp.* 1 Cor. 2. 1–10 *also* John 14. 18–23	*or* Isa. 45. 6b–8, 18, 21b–end Ps. 85. 7–end Luke 7. 18b–23	Ps. *75*; 96 *alt.* Ps. 119. 57–80 Isa. 51. 1–8
	Pw			2 Thess. ch. 1
15	Th		Isa. 54. 1–10 Ps. 30. 1–5, 11–end Luke 7. 24–30	Ps. *76*; 97 *alt.* Ps. 56; *57*; (63†) Isa. 51. 9–16
	P			2 Thess. ch. 2
16	F		Isa. 56. 1–3a, 6–8 Ps. 67 John 5. 33–36	Ps. 77; *98* *alt.* Ps. *51*; 54 Isa. 51. 17–end
	P			2 Thess. ch. 3

*For Ember Day provision, see p. 11.

Second Service Evening Prayer	Calendar and Holy Communion	Morning Prayer	Evening Prayer
Ps. *11*; 12; 13 *alt.* Ps. 33 Isa. 30. 19–end Matt. 14. 13–end Pw	**Nicholas, Bishop of Myra, c. 326** Com. Bishop	Isa. ch. 46 I Thess. 2. 1–12	Isa. 30. 19–end Matt. 14. 13–end
Ps. *10*; 14 *alt.* Ps. 119. 33–56 Isa. ch. 31 Matt. 15. 1–20 P		Isa. ch. 47 I Thess. 2. 13–end	Isa. ch. 31 Matt. 15. 1–20
Ps. 73 *alt.* Ps. 39; **40** Isa. ch. 32 Matt. 15. 21–28 Pw	**The Conception of the Blessed Virgin Mary** Isa. 48. 1–11 I Thess. ch. 3	Isa. ch. 32 Matt. 15. 21–28
Ps. 82; **90** *alt.* Ps. 35 Isa. 33. 1–22 Matt. 15. 29–end P		Isa. 48. 12–end I Thess. 4. 1–12	Isa. 33. 1–22 Matt. 15. 29–end
Ps. 93; **94** *alt.* Ps. 45; **46** Isa. ch. 35 Matt. 16. 1–12 ct P		Isa. 49. 1–13 I Thess. 4. 13–end	Isa. ch. 35 Matt. 16. 1–12 ct
Ps. 12; [14] Isa. 5. 8–end Acts 13. 13–41 *Gospel:* John 5. 31–40 P	THE THIRD SUNDAY IN ADVENT Isa. ch. 35 Ps. 80. 1–7 I Cor. 4. 1–5 Matt. 11. 2–10	Ps. 68. 1–19 Zeph. 3. 14–end James 5. 7–10	Ps. 12; [14] Isa. 5. 8–end Acts 13. 13–41
Ps. 25; **26** *alt.* Ps. **47**; 49 Isa. 38. 1–8, 21–22 Matt. 16. 13–end P		Isa. 49. 14–25 I Thess. 5. 1–11	Isa. 38. 1–8, 21–22 Matt. 16. 13–end
Ps. **50**; 54 *alt.* Ps. 50 Isa. 38. 9–20 Matt. 17. 1–13 Pr	**Lucy, Martyr at Syracuse, 304** Com. Virgin Martyr	Isa. ch. 50 I Thess. 5. 12–end	Isa. 38. 9–20 Matt. 17. 1–13
Ps. 25; **82** *alt.* Ps. **59**; 60; (67) Isa. ch. 39 Matt. 17. 14–21 P	Ember Day Ember CEG	Isa. 51. 1–8 2 Thess. ch. 1	Isa. ch. 39 Matt. 17. 14–21
Ps. 44 *alt.* Ps. 61; **62**; 64 Zeph. 1.1 – 2.3 Matt. 17. 22–end P		Isa. 51. 9–16 2 Thess. ch. 2	Zeph. 1.1 – 2.3 Matt. 17. 22–end
Ps. 49 *alt.* Ps. 38 Zeph. 3. 1–13 Matt. 18. 1–20 P	O Sapientia Ember Day Ember CEG	Isa. 51. 17–end 2 Thess. ch. 3	Zeph. 3. 1–13 Matt. 18. 1–20

December 2016

		Sunday Principal Service Weekday Eucharist	Third Service Morning Prayer

17	Sa	O Sapientia* *Eglantyne Jebb, Social Reformer, Founder of Save the Children, 1928* Isa. 7. 10–14 Ps. 24. 1–6 Luke 1. 26–38	
		Gen. 49. 2, 8–10 Ps. 72. 1–5, 18–19 Matt. 1. 1–17	Ps. 71 *alt.* Ps. 68 Isa. 52. 1–12
	P		Jude
18	S	THE FOURTH SUNDAY OF ADVENT	
		Isa. 7. 10–16 Ps. 80. 1–8, 18–end (*or* 80. 1–8) Rom. 1. 1–7	Ps. 144 Micah 5. 2–5a Luke 1. 26–38
	P	Matt. 1. 18–end	
19	M	Judg. 13. 2–7, 24–end Ps. 71. 3–8	Ps. 144; *146* Isa. 52.13 – 53.end
	P	Luke 1. 5–25	2 Pet. 1. 1–15
20	Tu	Isa. 7. 10–14 Ps. 24. 1–6 Luke 1. 26–38	Ps. *46*; 95 Isa. ch. 54 2 Pet. 1.16. – 2.3
	P		
21	W**		
		Zeph. 3. 14–18 Ps. 33. 1–4, 11–12, 20–end Luke 1. 39–45	Ps. *121*; 122; 123 Isa. ch. 55
	P		2 Pet. 2. 4–end
22	Th	1 Sam. 1. 24–end Ps. 113	Ps. *124*; 125; 126; 127 Isa. 56. 1–8
	P	Luke 1. 46–56	2 Pet. ch. 3
23	F	Mal. 3. 1–4; 4. 5–end Ps. 25. 3–9	Ps. 128; 129; *130*; 131 Isa. 63. 1–6
	P	Luke 1. 57–66	2 John
24	Sa	CHRISTMAS EVE	
		Morning Eucharist 2 Sam. 7. 1–5, 8–11, 16 Ps. 89. 2, 19–27 Acts 13. 16–26 Luke 1. 67–79	Ps. *45*; 113 Isa. ch. 58 3 John
	P		
25	S	**CHRISTMAS DAY** *Any of the following sets of readings may be used on the evening of Christmas Eve and on Christmas Day. Set III should be used at some service during the celebration.*	
		I Isa. 9. 2–7 Ps. 96 Titus 2. 11–14 Luke 2. 1–14 [15–20]	MP: Ps. *110*; 117 Isa. 62. 1–5 Matt. 1. 18–end
		II Isa. 62. 6–end Ps. 97 Titus 3. 4–7 Luke 2. [1–7] 8–20	
	℗	III Isa. 52. 7–10 Ps. 98 Heb. 1. 1–4 [5–12] John 1. 1–14	

*Evening Prayer readings from the Additional Weekday Lectionary (see p. 92) may be used from 17 to 23 December.
**Thomas the Apostle may be celebrated on 21 December instead of 3 July.

Second Service Evening Prayer	Calendar and Holy Communion	Morning Prayer	Evening Prayer
Ps. 42; *43* *alt.* Ps. 65; *66* Zeph. 3. 14–end Matt. 18. 21–end **ct**	Ember Day Ember CEG **P**	Isa. 52. 1–12 Jude	Zeph. 3. 14–end Matt. 18. 21–end **ct**
Ps. 113; [126] 1 Sam. 1. 1–20 Rev. 22. 6–end *Gospel:* Luke 1. 39–45	**THE FOURTH SUNDAY IN ADVENT** Isa. 40. 1–9 Ps. 145. 17–end Phil. 4. 4–7 John 1. 19–28 **P**	Ps. 144 Micah 5. 2–5a Luke 1. 26–38	Ps. 113; [126] 1 Sam. 1. 1–20 Rev. 22. 6–end
Ps. 10; *57* Mal. 1. 1, 6–end Matt. 19. 1–12	**P**	Isa. 52.13 – 53.end 2 Pet. 1. 1–15	Mal. 1. 1, 6–end Matt. 19. 1–12
Ps. *4*; 9 Mal. 2. 1–16 Matt. 19. 13–15	**P**	Isa. ch. 54 2 Pet. 1.16. – 2.3	Mal. 2. 1–16 Matt. 19. 13–15 *or First EP of Thomas* (Ps. 27) Isa. ch. 35 Heb. 10.35 – 11.1 **R ct**
Ps. 80; *84* Mal. 2.17 – 3.12 Matt. 19. 16–end	**THOMAS THE APOSTLE** Job 42. 1–6 Ps. 139. 1–11 Eph. 2. 19–end John 20. 24–end **R**	(Ps. 92; 146) 2 Sam. 15. 17–21 or Ecclus. ch. 2 John 11. 1–16	(Ps. 139) Hab. 2. 1–4 1 Pet. 1. 3–12
Ps. 24; *48* Mal. 3.13 – 4.end Matt. 23. 1–12	**P**	Isa. 56. 1–8 2 Pet. ch. 3	Mal. 3.13 – 4.end Matt. 23. 1–12
Ps. 89. 1–37 Nahum ch. 1 Matt. 23. 13–28	**P**	Isa. 63. 1–6 2 John	Nahum ch. 1 Matt. 23. 13–28
Ps. 85 Zech. ch. 2 Rev. 1. 1–8	**CHRISTMAS EVE** Collect (1) Christmas Eve (2) Advent 1 Mic. 5. 2–5a Ps. 24 Titus 3. 3–7 Luke 2. 1–14 **P**	Isa. ch. 58 3 John	Zech. ch. 2 Rev. 1. 1–8
EP: Ps. 8 Isa. 65. 17–25 Phil. 2. 5–11 *or* Luke 2. 1–20 *if it has not been used at the* *principal service of the day*	**CHRISTMAS DAY** Isa. 9. 2–7 Ps. 98 Heb. 1. 1–12 John 1. 1–14	Ps. 110; 117 Isa. 62. 1–5 Matt. 1. 18–end	Ps. 8 Isa. 65. 17–25 Phil. 2. 5–11 *or* Luke 2. 1–20

December 2016

			Sunday Principal Service / Weekday Eucharist	Third Service / Morning Prayer

26 M   STEPHEN, DEACON, FIRST MARTYR

> 2 Chron. 24. 20–22
> or Acts 7. 51–end
> Ps. 119. 161–168
> Acts 7. 51–end
> or Gal. 2. 16b–20
> Matt. 10. 17–22

> MP: Ps. *13*; 31. 1–8; 150
> Jer. 26. 12–15
> Acts ch. 6

R

27 Tu   JOHN, APOSTLE AND EVANGELIST

> Exod. 33. 7–11a
> Ps. 117
> 1 John ch. 1
> John 21. 19b–end

> MP: Ps. *21*; 147. 13–end
> Exod. 33. 12–end
> 1 John 2. 1–11

W

28 W   THE HOLY INNOCENTS

> Jer. 31. 15–17
> Ps. 124
> 1 Cor. 1. 26–29
> Matt. 2. 13–18

> MP: Ps. *36*; 146
> Baruch 4. 21–27
> or Gen. 37. 13–20
> Matt. 18. 1–10

R

29 Th   **Thomas Becket, Archbishop of Canterbury, Martyr, 1170***
Com. Martyr   *or*   1 John 2. 3–11
esp. Matt. 10. 28–33   Ps. 96. 1–4
Wr   *also* Ecclus. 51. 1–8   Luke 2. 22–35

> Ps. *19*; 20
> Isa. 57. 15–end
> John 1. 1–18

30 F

> 1 John 2. 12–17
> Ps. 96. 7–10
> Luke 2. 36–40

> Ps. 111; 112; *113*
> Isa. 59. 1–15a
> John 1. 19–28

W

31 Sa   *John Wyclif, Reformer, 1384*

> 1 John 2. 18–21
> Ps. 96. 1, 11–end
> John 1. 1–18

> Ps. 102
> Isa. 59. 15b–end
> John 1. 29–34

W

January 2017

1 S   THE NAMING AND CIRCUMCISION OF JESUS (*or transferred to the 2nd*)

> Num. 6. 22–end
> Ps. 8
> Gal. 4. 4–7
> Luke 2. 15–21

> MP: Ps. *103*; 150
> Gen. 17. 1–13
> Rom. 2. 17–end

W

or, for The Second Sunday of Christmas:

> Isa. 63. 7–9
> Ps. 148 (or 148. 7–end)
> Heb. 2. 10–end
> Matt. 2. 13–end

> Ps. 105. 1–11
> Isa. 35. 1–6
> Gal. 2. 23–end

W

2 M   For The Naming and Circumcision of Jesus, see the 1st.
Basil the Great and Gregory of Nazianzus, Bishops, Teachers, 379 and 389
Seraphim, Monk of Sarov, Spiritual Guide, 1833; Vedanayagam Samuel Azariah, Bishop in South India, Evangelist, 1945
Com. Teacher   *or*   1 John 2. 22–28
esp. 2 Tim. 4. 1–8   Ps. 98. 1–4
W   Matt. 5. 13–19   John 1. 19–28

> Ps. 18. 1–30
> Isa. 60. 1–12
> John 1. 35–42

*Thomas Becket may be celebrated on 7 July instead of 29 December.

Second Service Evening Prayer		Calendar and Holy Communion	Morning Prayer	Evening Prayer
EP: Ps. 57; *86* Gen. 4. 1–10 Matt. 23. 34–end	R	**STEPHEN, DEACON, FIRST MARTYR** Collect (1) Stephen (2) Christmas 2 Chron. 24. 20–22 Ps. 119. 161–168 Acts 7. 55–end Matt. 23. 34–end	(Ps. 13; 31. 1–8; 150) Jer. 26. 12–15 Acts ch. 6	(Ps. 57; 86) Gen. 4. 1–10 Matt. 10. 17–22
EP: Ps. 97 Isa. 6. 1–8 1 John 5. 1–12	W	**JOHN, APOSTLE AND EVANGELIST** Collect (1) John (2) Christmas Exod. 33. 18–end Ps. 92. 11–end 1 John ch. 1 John 21. 19b–end	(Ps. 21; 147. 13–end) Exod. 33. 7–11a 1 John 2. 1–11	(Ps. 97) Isa. 6. 1–8 1 John 5. 1–12
EP: Ps. 123; *128* Isa. 49. 14–25 Mark 10. 13–16	R	**THE HOLY INNOCENTS** Collect (1) Innocents (2) Christmas Jer. 31. 10–17 Ps. 123 Rev. 14. 1–5 Matt. 2. 13–18	(Ps. 36; 146) Baruch 4. 21–27 or Gen. 37. 13–20 Matt. 18. 1–10	(Ps. 124; 128) Isa. 49. 14–25 Mark 10. 13–16
Ps. 131; *132* Jonah ch. 1 Col. 1. 1–14	W	CEG of Christmas	Isa. 57. 15–end John 1. 1–18	Jonah ch. 1 Col. 1. 1–14
Ps. *65*; 84 Jonah ch. 2 Col. 1. 15–23	W	CEG of Christmas	Isa. 59. 1–15a John 1. 19–28	Jonah ch. 2 Col. 1. 15–23
Ps. *90*; 148 Jonah chs 3 & 4 Col. 1.24 – 2.7 or First EP of The Naming of Jesus Ps. 148 Jer. 23. 1–6 Col. 2. 8–15 ct	W	**Silvester, Bishop of Rome, 335** Com. Bishop	Isa. 59. 15b–end John 1. 29–34	Jonah chs 3 & 4 Col. 1.24 – 2.7 or First EP of The Circumcision of Christ (Ps. 148) Jer. 23. 1–6 Col. 2. 8–15 ct
EP: Ps. 115 Deut. 30. [1–10] 11–end Acts 3. 1–16	W	**THE CIRCUMCISION OF CHRIST** (*or transferred to the 2nd*) Additional collect Gen. 17. 3b–10 Ps. 98 Rom. 4. 8–13 or Eph. 2. 11–18 Luke 2. 15–21	Ps. 103; 150 Gen. 17. 1–13 Rom. 2. 17–end	Ps. 115 Deut. 30. [1–10] 11–end Acts 3. 1–16
Ps. 132 Isa. 49. 7–13 Phil. 2. 1–11 *Gospel:* Luke 2. 41–52	W	*or, for The Sunday after Christmas Day:* Isa. 62. 10–12 Ps. 45. 1–7 Gal. 4. 1–7 Matt. 1. 18–end	Ps. 105. 1–11 Isa. 35. 1–6 Gal. 2. 23–end	Ps. 132 Isa. 49. 7–13 Phil. 2. 1–11
Ps. 45; *46* Ruth ch. 1 Col. 2. 8–end	W		Isa. 60. 1–12 John 1. 35–42	Ruth ch. 1 Col. 2. 8–end

January 2017

		Sunday Principal Service / Weekday Eucharist	Third Service / Morning Prayer
3	Tu	1 John 2.29 – 3.6 Ps. 98. 2–7	Ps. *127*; 128; 131 Isa. 60. 13–end
	W	John 1. 29–34	John 1. 43–end
4	W	1 John 3. 7–10 Ps. 98. 1, 8–end	Ps. 89. 1–37 Isa. ch. 61
	W	John 1. 35–42	John 2. 1–12
5	Th	1 John 3. 11–21 Ps. 100	Ps. 8; *48* Isa. ch. 62
		John 1. 43–end	John 2. 13–end
	W		
6	F	**THE EPIPHANY**	
		Isa. 60. 1–6 Ps. 72. 1–15 (or 72. 10–15) Eph. 3. 1–12	*MP*: Ps. 132; 113 Jer. 31. 7–14 John 1. 29–34
	♰	Matt. 2. 1–12	
		or, if The Epiphany is celebrated on 8 January: 1 John 5. 5–13 Ps. 147. 13–end	Ps. *46*; 147. 13–end Isa. 63. 7–end
	W	Mark 1. 7–11	1 John ch. 3
7	Sa	1 John 3.22 – 4.6 Ps. 2. 7–end Matt. 4. 12–17, 23–end	Ps. *99*; 147. 1–12 *alt.* Ps. *76*; 79* Isa. 63. 7–end 1 John ch. 3
	W		
		or, if The Epiphany is celebrated on 8 January: 1 John 5. 14–end Ps. 149. 1–5	Ps. *99*; 147. 1–12 Isa. ch. 64
	W	John 2. 1–11	1 John 4. 7–end
8	S	**THE BAPTISM OF CHRIST (THE FIRST SUNDAY OF EPIPHANY)** (*or transferred to 9 January if The Epiphany is celebrated today. For The Epiphany, see provision on the 5th and 6th*)	
		Isa. 42. 1–9 Ps. 29 Acts 10. 34–43	Ps. 89. 19–29 Exod. 14. 15–22 1 John 5. 6–9
	♰	Matt. 3. 13–end	
9 DEL 1	M	For The Baptism, see provision on the 8th. Heb. 1. 1–6 Ps. 97. 1–2, 6–10	Ps. *2*; 110 *alt.* Ps. *80*; 82 Amos ch. 1
	W	Mark 1. 14–20	1 Cor. 1. 1–17
10	Tu	*William Laud, Archbishop of Canterbury, 1645* Heb. 2. 5–12 Ps. 8	Ps. 8; *9* *alt.* Ps. 87; *89. 1–18* Amos ch. 2
	W	Mark 1. 21–28	1 Cor. 1. 18–end
11	W	*Mary Slessor, Missionary in West Africa, 1915* Heb. 2. 14–end Ps. 105. 1–9	Ps. 19; *20* *alt.* Ps. 119. 105–128 Amos ch. 3
	W	Mark 1. 29–39	1 Cor. ch. 2

*Alt. psalm cycle begins on the 9th if The Epiphany is celebrated on the 8th.

Second Service Evening Prayer	Calendar and Holy Communion	Morning Prayer	Evening Prayer
Ps. **2**; 110 Ruth ch. 2 Col. 3. 1–11	**W**	Isa. 60. 13–end John 1. 43–end	Ruth ch. 2 Col. 3. 1–11
Ps. 85; **87** Ruth ch. 3 Col. 3.12 – 4.1	**W**	Isa. ch. 61 John 2. 1–12	Ruth ch. 3 Col. 3.12 – 4.1
First EP of The Epiphany Ps. 96; **97** Isa. 49. 1–13 John 4. 7–26 ℣ **ct** *or, if The Epiphany is celebrated on 8 January:* Ps. 96; **97** Ruth 4. 1–17 Col. 4. 2–end	**W**	Isa. ch. 62 John 2. 13–end	*First EP of The Epiphany* Ps. 96; **97** Isa. 49. 1–13 John 4. 7–26 ℣ **ct**
EP: Ps. 98; 100 Baruch 4.36 – 5.end *or* Isa. 60. 1–9 John 2. 1–11 Ps. 145 Bar. 1.15 – 2.10 *or* Jer. 23. 1–8 Matt. 20. 1–16	**THE EPIPHANY** Isa. 60. 1–9 Ps. 100 Eph. 3. 1–12 Matt. 2. 1–12 ℣	Ps. 132; 113 Jer. 31. 7–14 John 1. 29–34	Ps. 72; 98 Baruch 4.36 – 5.end *or* Isa. 60. 1–9 John 2. 1–11
First EP of The Baptism of Christ Ps. 36 Isa. ch. 61 Titus 2. 11–14; 3. 4–7 ℣ **ct** *First EP of The Epiphany* Ps. 96; **97** Isa. 49. 1–13 John 4. 7–26 ℣ **ct**	**W** *or* **G**	Isa. 63. 7–end 1 John ch. 3	Bar. 1.15 – 2.10 *or* Jer. 23. 1–8 Matt. 20. 1–16 **ct**
	THE FIRST SUNDAY AFTER THE EPIPHANY To celebrate The Baptism of Christ, see *Common Worship* provision.		
Ps. 46; 47 Josh. 3. 1–8, 14–end Heb. 1. 1–12 *Gospel:* Luke 3. 15–22	Zech. 8. 1–8 Ps. 72. 1–8 Rom. 12. 1–5 Luke 2. 41–end **W** *or* **G**	Ps. 89. 19–29 Exod. 14. 15–22 1 John 5. 6–9	Ps. 46; 47 Josh. 3. 1–8, 14–end Heb. 1. 1–12
Ps. **34**; 36 *alt.* Ps. **85**; 86 Gen. 1. 1–19 Matt. 21. 1–17	**W** *or* **G**	Amos ch. 1 1 Cor. 1. 1–17	Gen. 1. 1–19 Matt. 21. 1–17
Ps. **45**; 46 *alt.* Ps. 89. 19–end Gen. 1.20 – 2.3 Matt. 21. 18–32	**W** *or* **G**	Amos ch. 2 1 Cor. 1. 18–end	Gen. 1.20 – 2.3 Matt. 21. 18–32
Ps. **47**; 48 *alt.* Ps. **91**; 93 Gen. 2. 4–end Matt. 21. 33–end	**W** *or* **G**	Amos ch. 3 1 Cor. ch. 2	Gen. 2. 4–end Matt. 21. 33–end

January 2017

		Sunday Principal Service / Weekday Eucharist	Third Service / Morning Prayer

12 Th
Aelred of Hexham, Abbot of Rievaulx, 1167
Benedict Biscop, Abbot of Wearmouth, Scholar, 689
Com. Religious   or   Heb. 3. 7–14
also Ecclus. 15. 1–6   Ps. 95. 1, 8–end
                                                 Mark 1. 40–end

Ps. *21*; 24
alt. Ps. 90; **92**
Amos ch. 4
1 Cor. ch. 3

W

13 F
Hilary, Bishop of Poitiers, Teacher, 367
Kentigern (Mungo), Missionary Bishop in Strathclyde and Cumbria, 603; George Fox, Founder of the Society of Friends (the Quakers), 1691
Com. Teacher   or   Heb. 4. 1–5, 11
also 1 John 2. 18–25   Ps. 78. 3–8
John 8. 25–32   Mark 2. 1–12

Ps. *67*; 72
alt. Ps. **88**; (95)
Amos 5. 1–17
1 Cor. ch. 4

W

14 Sa
Heb. 4. 12–end
Ps. 19. 7–end
Mark 2. 13–17

Ps. 29; **33**
alt. Ps. 96; **97**; 100
Amos 5. 18–end
1 Cor. ch. 5

W

15 S
THE SECOND SUNDAY OF EPIPHANY
Isa. 49. 1–7
Ps. 40. 1–12
1 Cor. 1. 1–9
John 1. 29–42

Ps. 145. 1–12
Jer. 1. 4–10
Mark 1. 14–20

W

16 M
DEL 2
Heb. 5. 1–10
Ps. 110. 1–4
Mark 2. 18–22

Ps. 145; **146**
alt. Ps. **98**; 99; 101
Amos ch. 6
1 Cor. 6. 1–11

W

17 Tu
Antony of Egypt, Hermit, Abbot, 356
Charles Gore, Bishop, Founder of the Community of the Resurrection, 1932
Com. Religious   or   Heb. 6. 10–end
esp. Phil. 3. 7–14   Ps. 111
also Matt. 19. 16–26   Mark 2. 23–end

Ps. *132*; 147. 1–12
alt. Ps. 106† (or Ps. 103)
Amos ch. 7
1 Cor. 6. 12–end

W

18 W
The Week of Prayer for Christian Unity until 25th
Amy Carmichael, Founder of the Dohnavur Fellowship, Spiritual Writer, 1951
Heb. 7. 1–3, 15–17
Ps. 110. 1–4
Mark 3. 1–6

Ps. *81*; 147. 13–end
alt. Ps. 110; *111*; 112
Amos ch. 8
1 Cor. 7. 1–24

W

19 Th
Wulfstan, Bishop of Worcester, 1095
Com. Bishop   or   Heb. 7.25 – 8.6
esp. Matt. 24. 42–46   Ps. 40. 7–10, 17–end
                                                 Mark 3. 7–12

Ps. *76*; 148
alt. Ps. 113; **115**
Amos ch. 9
1 Cor. 7. 25–end

W

20 F
Richard Rolle of Hampole, Spiritual Writer, 1349
Heb. 8. 6–end
Ps. 85. 7–end
Mark 3. 13–19

Ps. *27*; 149
alt. Ps. 139
Hos. 1.1 – 2.1
1 Cor. ch. 8

W

21 Sa
Agnes, Child Martyr at Rome, 304
Com. Martyr   or   Heb. 9. 2–3, 11–14
also Rev. 7. 13–end   Ps. 47. 1–8
                                                 Mark 3. 20–21

Ps. *122*; 128; 150
alt. Ps. 120; *121*; 122
Hos. 2. 2–17
1 Cor. 9. 1–14

Wr

Second Service Evening Prayer	Calendar and Holy Communion	Morning Prayer	Evening Prayer
Ps. *61*; 65 *alt.* Ps. 94 Gen. ch. 3 Matt. 22. 1–14	W *or* G	Amos ch. 4 I Cor. ch. 3	Gen. ch. 3 Matt. 22. 1–14
	Hilary, Bishop of Poitiers, Teacher, 367 Com. Doctor		
Ps. 68 *alt.* Ps. 102 Gen. 4. 1–16, 25–26 Matt. 22. 15–33	W *or* Gw	Amos 5. 1–17 I Cor. ch. 4	Gen. 4. 1–16, 25–26 Matt. 22. 15–33
Ps. 84; *85* *alt.* Ps. 104 Gen. 6. 1–10 Matt. 22. 34–end ct	W *or* G	Amos 5. 18–end I Cor. ch. 5	Gen. 6. 1–10 Matt. 22. 34–end ct
Ps. 96 Ezek. 2.1 – 3.4 Gal. 1. 11–end *Gospel:* John 1. 43–end	THE SECOND SUNDAY AFTER THE EPIPHANY 2 Kings 4. 1–17 Ps. 107. 13–22 Rom. 12. 6–16a John 2. 1–11 W *or* G	Ps. 145. 1–12 Jer. 1. 4–10 Mark 1. 14–20	Ps. 96 Ezek. 2.1 – 3.4 Gal. 1. 11–end
Ps. 71 *alt.* Ps. 105† (*or* Ps. 103) Gen. 6.11 – 7.10 Matt. 24. 1–14	W *or* G	Amos ch. 6 I Cor. 6. 1–11	Gen. 6.11 – 7.10 Matt. 24. 1–14
Ps. 89. 1–37 *alt.* Ps. 107† Gen. 7. 11–end Matt. 24. 15–28	W *or* G	Amos ch. 7 I Cor. 6. 12–end	Gen. 7. 11–end Matt. 24. 15–28
Ps. *97*; 98 *alt.* Ps. 119. 129–152 Gen. 8. 1–14 Matt. 24. 29–end	**Prisca, Martyr at Rome, c. 265** For the Week of Prayer for Christian Unity, see *Common Worship* provision. Com. Virgin Martyr Wr *or* Gr	Amos ch. 8 I Cor. 7. 1–24	Gen. 8. 1–14 Matt. 24. 29–end
Ps. 99; 100; *111* *alt.* Ps. 114; *116*; 117 Gen. 8.15 – 9.7 Matt. 25. 1–13	W *or* G	Amos ch. 9 I Cor. 7. 25–end	Gen. 8.15 – 9.7 Matt. 25. 1–13
Ps. 73 *alt.* Ps. *130*; 131; 137 Gen. 9. 8–19 Matt. 25. 14–30	**Fabian, Bishop of Rome, Martyr, 250** Com. Martyr Wr *or* Gr	Hos. 1.1 – 2.1 I Cor. ch. 8	Gen. 9. 8–19 Matt. 25. 14–30
Ps. *61*; 66 *alt.* Ps. 118 Gen. 11. 1–9 Matt. 25. 31–end ct	**Agnes, Child Martyr at Rome, 304** Com. Virgin Martyr Wr *or* Gr	Hos. 2. 2–17 I Cor. 9. 1–14	Gen. 11. 1–9 Matt. 25. 31–end ct

January 2017

			Sunday Principal Service Weekday Eucharist	Third Service Morning Prayer

22 S — THE THIRD SUNDAY OF EPIPHANY

	Isa. 9. 1–4	Ps. 113
	Ps. 27. 1, 4–12 (or 27. 1–11)	Amos 3. 1–8
	1 Cor. 1. 10–18	1 John 1. 1–4
	Matt. 4. 12–23	

W

23 M

DEL 3

	Heb. 9. 15, 24–end	Ps. 40; *108*
	Ps. 98. 1–7	alt. Ps. 123; 124; 125; *126*
	Mark 3. 22–30	Hos. 2.18 – 3.end
		1 Cor. 9. 15–end

W

24 Tu   **Francis de Sales, Bishop of Geneva, Teacher, 1274**

Com. Teacher	or	Heb. 10. 1–10	Ps. 34; *36*
also Prov. 3. 13–18		Ps. 40. 1–4, 7–10	alt. Ps. *132*; 133
John 3. 17–21		Mark 3. 31–end	Hos. 4. 1–16
			1 Cor. 10. 1–13

W

W

25 W — THE CONVERSION OF PAUL

	Jer. 1. 4–10	*MP*: Ps. 66; 147. 13–end
	or Acts 9. 1–22	Ezek. 3. 22–end
	Ps. 67	Phil. 3. 1–14
	Acts 9. 1–22	
	or Gal. 1. 11–16a	
	Matt. 19. 27–end	

W

26 Th   **Timothy and Titus, Companions of Paul**

Isa. 61. 1–3a	or	Heb. 10. 19–25	Ps. *47*; 48
Ps. 100		Ps. 24. 1–6	alt. Ps. *143*; 146
2 Tim. 2. 1–8		Mark 4. 21–25	Hos. 5.8 – 6.6
or Titus 1. 1–5			1 Cor. 11. 2–16
Luke 10. 1–9			

W

27 F

	Heb. 10. 32–end	Ps. 61; *65*
	Ps. 37. 3–6, 40–end	alt. Ps. 142; *144*
	Mark 4. 26–34	Hos. 6.7 – 7.2
		1 Cor. 11. 17–end

W

28 Sa   **Thomas Aquinas, Priest, Philosopher, Teacher, 1274**

Com. Teacher	or	Heb. 11. 1–2, 8–19	Ps. 68
esp. Wisd. 7. 7–10, 15–16		*Canticle*: Luke 1. 69–73	alt. Ps. 147
1 Cor. 2. 9–end		Mark 4. 35–end	Hos. ch. 8
John 16. 12–15			1 Cor. 12. 1–11

W

29 S — THE FOURTH SUNDAY OF EPIPHANY
or The Presentation of Christ in the Temple*

	1 Kings 17. 8–16	Ps. 71. 1–6, 15–17
	Ps. 36. 5–10	Hag. 2. 1–9
	1 Cor. 1. 18–end	1 Cor. 3. 10–17
	John 2. 1–11	

W

30 M   **Charles, King and Martyr, 1649**

DEL 4

Com. Martyr	or	Heb. 11. 32–end	Ps. *57*; 96
also Ecclus. 2. 12–17		Ps. 31. 19–end	alt. Ps. *1*; 2; 3***
1 Tim. 6. 12–16		Mark 5. 1–20	Hos. ch. 9
Wr [Gr]**			1 Cor. 12. 12–end

*See provision for First EP on 1 February and throughout the day for The Presentation on 2 February.
**Ordinary Time begins today if The Presentation was observed on the 29th.
***If The Presentation was observed on the 29th, the alternative psalms are used this week.

Second Service Evening Prayer	Calendar and Holy Communion	Morning Prayer	Evening Prayer
	THE THIRD SUNDAY AFTER THE EPIPHANY		
Ps. 33 (or 33.1–12) Eccles. 3. 1–11 I Pet. 1. 3–12 *Gospel*: Luke 4. 14–21	2 Kings 6. 14b–23 Ps. 102. 15–22 Rom. 12. 16b–end Matt. 8. 1–13 W *or* **G**	Ps. 113 Amos 3. 1–8 I John 1. 1–4	Ps. 33 (or 33.1–12) Eccles. 3. 1–11 I Pet. 1. 3–12
Ps. *138*; 144 *alt.* Ps. *127*; 128; 129 Gen. 11.27 – 12.9 Matt. 26. 1–16	 W *or* **G**	Hos. 2.18 – 3.end I Cor. 9. 15–end	Gen. 11.27 – 12.9 Matt. 26. 1–16
Ps. 145 *alt.* Ps. (134); *135* Gen. 13. 2–end Matt. 26. 17–35 *or First EP of The Conversion of Paul* Ps. 149 Isa. 49. 1–13 Acts 22. 3–16 ct	 W *or* **G**	Hos. 4. 1–16 I Cor. 10. 1–13	Gen. 13. 2–end Matt. 26. 17–35 *or First EP of The Conversion of Paul* (Ps. 149) Isa. 49. 1–13 Acts 22. 3–16 **W ct**
	THE CONVERSION OF PAUL		
EP: Ps. 119. 41–56 Ecclus. 39. 1–10 *or* Isa. 56. 1–8 Col. 1.24 – 2.7	Josh. 5. 13–end Ps. 67 Acts 9. 1–22 Matt. 19. 27–end W	(Ps. 66; 147. 13–end) Ezek. 3. 22–end Phil. 3. 1–14	(Ps. 119. 41–56) Ecclus. 39. 1–10 *or* Isa. 56. 1–8 Col. 1.24 – 2.7
Ps. *24*; 33 *alt.* Ps. *138*; 140; 141 Gen. ch. 15 Matt. 26. 47–56	 W *or* **G**	Hos. 5.8 – 6.6 I Cor. 11. 2–16	Gen. ch. 15 Matt. 26. 47–56
Ps. *67*; 77 *alt.* Ps. *145* Gen. ch. 16 Matt. 26.57–end	 W *or* **G**	Hos. 6.7 – 7.2 I Cor. 11. 17–end	Gen. ch. 16 Matt. 26.57–end
Ps. *72*; 76 *alt.* Ps. *148*; 149; 150 Gen. 17. 1–22 Matt. 27. 1–10 ct	 W *or* **G**	Hos. ch. 8 I Cor. 12. 1–11	Gen. 17. 1–22 Matt. 27. 1–10 ct
	THE FOURTH SUNDAY AFTER THE EPIPHANY		
Ps. 34 (or 34. 1–10) Gen. 28. 10–end Philemon 1–16 *Gospel*: Mark 1. 21–28	I Sam. 10. 17–24 Ps. 97 Rom. 13. 1–7 Matt. 8. 23–34 W *or* **G**	Ps. 71. 1–6, 15–17 Hag. 2. 1–9 I Cor. 3. 10–17	Ps. 34 (or 34. 1–10) Gen. 28. 10–end Philemon 1–16
	Charles, King and Martyr, 1649		
Ps. 2; *20* *alt.* Ps. *4*; 7 Gen. 18. 1–15 Matt. 27. 11–26	Com. Martyr W**r** *or* **G**r	Hos. ch. 9 I Cor. 12. 12–end	Gen. 18. 1–15 Matt. 27. 11–26

January 2017

			Sunday Principal Service Weekday Eucharist	Third Service Morning Prayer
31	Tu	*John Bosco, Priest, Founder of the Salesian Teaching Order, 1888*		
			Heb. 12. 1–4 Ps. 22. 25b–end Mark 5. 21–43	Ps. *93*; 97 *alt.* Ps. *5*; 6; (8) Hos. ch. 10
	W [G]			1 Cor. ch. 13

February 2017

1	W	*Brigid, Abbess of Kildare, c. 525*		
			Heb. 12. 4–7, 11–15 Ps. 103. 1–2, 13–18 Mark 6. 1–6a	Ps. *95*; 98 *alt.* Ps. 119. 1–32 Hos. 11. 1–11 1 Cor. 14. 1–19
	W [G]			
2	Th	**THE PRESENTATION OF CHRIST IN THE TEMPLE (CANDLEMAS)**		
			Mal. 3. 1–5 Ps. 24 (*or* 24. 7–end) Heb. 2. 14–end Luke 2. 22–40	*MP*: Ps. *48*; 146 Exod. 13. 1–16 Rom. 12. 1–5
	⅏	*or, if The Presentation is observed on 29 January:*		
	G		Heb. 12. 18–19, 21–24 Ps. 48. 1–3, 8–10 Mark 6. 7–13	Ps. 14; *15*; 16 Hos. 11.12 – 12.end 1 Cor. 14. 20–end
3	F	**Anskar, Archbishop of Hamburg, Missionary in Denmark and Sweden, 865** Ordinary Time starts today (or on 30 January if The Presentation is observed on 29 January)		
		Com. Missionary *esp.* Isa. 52. 7–10	*or* Heb. 13. 1–8 Ps. 27. 1–6, 9–12	Ps. 17; *19* Hos. 13. 1–14
	Gw	*also* Rom. 10. 11–15	Mark 6. 14–29	1 Cor. 16. 1–9
4	Sa	*Gilbert of Sempringham, Founder of the Gilbertine Order, 1189*		
			Heb. 13. 15–17, 20–21 Ps. 23 Mark 6. 30–34	Ps. 20; 21; *23* Hos. ch. 14 1 Cor. 16. 10–end
	G			
5	S	THE FOURTH SUNDAY BEFORE LENT **(Proper 1)**		
			Isa. 58. 1–9a [9b–12] Ps. 112 (*or* 112. 1–9) 1 Cor. 2. 1–12 [13–end] Matt. 5. 13–20	Ps. 5; 6 Jer. 26. 1–16 Acts 3. 1–10
	G			
6 DEL 5	M	*The Martyrs of Japan, 1597* (The Accession of Queen Elizabeth II may be observed on 6 February, and Collect, Readings and Post-Communion for the sovereign used.)		
			Gen. 1. 1–19 Ps. 104. 1–2, 6–13, 26 Mark 6. 53–end	Ps. 27; *30* Joel 1. 1–14 John 15. 1–11
	G			
7	Tu		Gen. 1.20 – 2.4a Ps. 8	Ps. 32; *36* Joel 1. 15–end
	G		Mark 7. 1–13	John 15. 12–17
8	W		Gen. 2. 4b–9, 15–17 Ps. 104. 11–12, 29–32	Ps. 34 Joel 2. 1–17
	G		Mark 7. 14–23	John 15. 18–end
9	Th		Gen. 2. 18–end Ps. 128	Ps. 37† Joel 2. 18–27
	G		Mark 7. 24–30	John 16. 1–15

Second Service Evening Prayer	Calendar and Holy Communion	Morning Prayer	Evening Prayer
Ps. *19*; 21 *alt.* Ps. *9*; 10† Gen. 18. 16–end Matt. 27. 27–44	**W** *or* **G**	Hos. ch. 10 I Cor. ch. 13	Gen. 18. 16–end Matt. 27. 27–44
First EP of The Presentation Ps. 118 I Sam. 1. 19b–end Heb. 4. 11–end 𝖂 **ct** *or, if The Presentation is observed on 29 January:* Ps. *11*; 12; 13 Gen. 19. 1–3, 12–29 Matt. 27. 45–56	**W** *or* **G**	Hos. 11. 1–11 I Cor. 14. 1–19	*First EP of The Presentation* Ps. 118 I Sam. 1. 19b–end Heb. 4. 11–end 𝖂 **ct**
	THE PRESENTATION OF CHRIST IN THE TEMPLE		
EP: Ps. 122; *132* Hag. 2. 1–9 John 2. 18–22	Mal. 3. 1–5 Ps. 48. 1–7 Gal. 4. 1–7 Luke 2. 22–40	Ps. 48; 146 Exod. 13. 1–16 Rom. 12. 1–5	Ps. 122; 132 Hag. 2. 1–9 John 2. 18–22
Ps. 18 Gen. 21. 1–21 Matt. 27. 57–end	𝖂		
	Blasius, Bishop of Sebastopol, Martyr, c. 316 Com. Martyr		
Ps. 22 Gen. 22. 1–19 Matt. 28. 1–15	**Gr**	Hos. 13. 1–14 I Cor. 16. 1–9	Gen. 22. 1–19 Matt. 28. 1–15
Ps. *24*; 25 Gen. ch. 23 Matt. 28. 16–end **ct**	**G**	Hos. ch. 14 I Cor. 16. 10–end	Gen. ch. 23 Matt. 28. 16–end **ct**
	THE FIFTH SUNDAY AFTER THE EPIPHANY		
Ps. [1; 3] 4 Amos 2. 4–end Eph. 4. 17–end *Gospel:* Mark 1. 29–39	Hos. 6. 4–6 Ps. 118. 14–21 Col. 3. 12–17 Matt. 13. 24b–30 **G**	Ps. 5; 6 Jer. 26. 1–16 Acts 3. 1–10	Ps. [1; 3] 4 Amos 2. 4–end Eph. 4. 17–end
	The Accession of Queen Elizabeth II, 1952 *For Accession Service:* Ps. 20; 101; 121; Josh. 1. 1–9; Prov. 8. 1–16; Rom. 13. 1–10; Rev. 21.22 – 22.4		
Ps. 26; *28*; 29 Lev. 19. 1–18, 30–end I Tim. 1. 1–17	*For The Accession:* I Pet. 2. 11–17 Matt. 22. 16–22 **G**	Joel 1. 1–14 John 15. 1–11	Lev. 19. 1–18, 30–end I Tim. 1. 1–17
Ps. 33 Lev. 23. 1–22 I Tim. 1.18 – 2.end	**G**	Joel 1. 15–end John 15. 12–17	Lev. 23. 1–22 I Tim. 1.18 – 2.end
Ps. 119. 33–56 Lev. 23. 23–end I Tim. ch. 3	**G**	Joel 2. 1–17 John 15. 18–end	Lev. 23. 23–end I Tim. ch. 3
Ps. 39; *40* Lev. 24. 1–9 I Tim. ch. 4	**G**	Joel 2. 18–27 John 16. 1–15	Lev. 24. 1–9 I Tim. ch. 4

February 2017

		Sunday Principal Service / Weekday Eucharist	Third Service / Morning Prayer

10	F	*Scholastica, sister of Benedict, Abbess of Plombariola, c. 543*	
		Gen. 3. 1–8	Ps. 31
	G	Ps. 32. 1–8	Joel 2. 28–end
		Mark 7. 31–end	John 16. 16–22
11	Sa	Gen. 3. 9–end	Ps. 41; *42*; 43
		Ps. 90. 1–12	Joel 3. 1–3, 9–end
	G	Mark 8. 1–10	John 16. 23–end
12	S	THE THIRD SUNDAY BEFORE LENT **(Proper 2)**	
		Deut. 30. 15–end	Ps. 10
		or Ecclus. 15. 15–end	Jer. 30. 1–3, 10–22
		Ps. 119. 1–8	Acts ch. 6
		I Cor. 3. 1–9	
	G	Matt. 5. 21–37	
13 DEL 6	M	Gen. 4. 1–15, 25	Ps. 44
		Ps. 50. 1, 8, 16–end	Eccles. ch. 1
	G	Mark 8. 11–13	John 17. 1–5
14	Tu	**Cyril and Methodius, Missionaries to the Slavs, 869 and 885**	
		Valentine, Martyr at Rome, c. 269	
		Com. Missionaries *or*	Gen. 6. 5–8; 7. 1–5, 10	Ps. *48*; 52
		esp. Isa. 52. 7–10	Ps. 29	Eccles. ch. 2
	Gw	*also* Rom. 10. 11–15	Mark 8. 14–21	John 17. 6–19
15	W	*Sigfrid, Bishop, Apostle of Sweden, 1045; Thomas Bray, Priest, Founder of the SPCK and the SPG, 1730*	
		Gen. 8. 6–13, 20–end	Ps. 119. 57–80
		Ps. 116. 10–end	Eccles. 3. 1–15
	G	Mark 8. 22–26	John 17. 20–end
16	Th	Gen. 9. 1–13	Ps. 56; *57*; (63†)
		Ps. 102. 16–23	Eccles. 3.16 – 4.end
	G	Mark 8. 27–33	John 18. 1–11
17	F	**Janani Luwum, Archbishop of Uganda, Martyr, 1977**	
		Com. Martyr *or*	Gen. 11. 1–9	Ps. *51*; 54
		also Ecclus. 4. 20–28	Ps. 33. 10–15	Eccles. ch. 5
	Gr	John 12. 24–32	Mark 8.34 – 9.1	John 18. 12–27
18	Sa	Heb. 11. 1–7	Ps. 68
		Ps. 145. 1–10	Eccles. ch. 6
	G	Mark 9. 2–13	John 18. 28–end
19	S	THE SECOND SUNDAY BEFORE LENT	
		Gen. 1.1 – 2.3	Ps. 100; 150
		Ps. 136 (*or* 136. 1–9, 23–end)	Job 38. 1–21
		Rom. 8. 18–25	Col. 1. 15–20
	G	Matt. 6. 25–end	
20 DEL 7	M	Ecclus. 1. 1–10	Ps. 71
		or James 1. 1–11	Eccles. 7. 1–14
		Ps. 93	John 19. 1–16
		or Ps. 119. 65–72	
	G	Mark 9. 14–29	
21	Tu	Ecclus. 2. 1–11	Ps. 73
		or James 1. 12–18	Eccles. 7. 15–end
		Ps. 37. 3–6, 27–28	John 19. 17–30
		or Ps. 94. 12–18	
	G	Mark 9. 30–37	
22	W	Ecclus. 4. 11–19	Ps. 77
		or James 1. 19–end	Eccles. ch. 8
		Ps. 119. 161–168	John 19. 31–end
		or Ps. 15	
	G	Mark 9. 38–40	

Second Service Evening Prayer	Calendar and Holy Communion	Morning Prayer	Evening Prayer
Ps. 35 Lev. 25. 1–24 I Tim. 5. 1–16	G	Joel 2. 28–end John 16. 16–22	Lev. 25. 1–24 I Tim. 5. 1–16
Ps. 45; **46** Num. 6. 1–5, 21–end I Tim. 5. 17–end **ct**	G	Joel 3. 1–3, 9–end John 16. 23–end	Num. 6. 1–5, 21–end I Tim. 5. 17–end **ct**
Ps. [7]; 13 Amos 3. 1–8 Eph. 5. 1–17 *Gospel:* Mark 1. 40–end	**SEPTUAGESIMA** Gen. 1. 1–5 Ps. 9. 10–20 I Cor. 9. 24–end Matt. 20. 1–16 G	Ps. 10 Jer. 30. 1–3, 10–22 Acts ch. 6	Ps. [7]; 13 Amos 3. 1–8 Eph. 5. 1–17
Ps. **47**; 49 Gen. 24. 1–28 I Tim. 6. 1–10	G	Eccles. ch. 1 John 17. 1–5	Gen. 24. 1–28 I Tim. 6. 1–10
Ps. 50 Gen. 24. 29–end I Tim. 6. 11–end	**Valentine, Martyr at Rome, c. 269** Com. Martyr Gr	Eccles. ch. 2 John 17. 6–19	Gen. 24. 29–end I Tim. 6. 11–end
Ps. **59**; 60; (67) Gen. 25. 7–11, 19–end 2 Tim. 1. 1–14	G	Eccles. 3. 1–15 John 17. 20–end	Gen. 25. 7–11, 19–end 2 Tim. 1. 1–14
61; **62**; 64 Gen. 26.34 – 27.40 2 Tim. 1.15 – 2.13	G	Eccles. 3.16 – 4.end John 18. 1–11	Gen. 26.34 – 27.40 2 Tim. 1.15 – 2.13
Ps. 38 Gen. 27.41 – 28.end 2 Tim. 2. 14–end	G	Eccles. ch. 5 John 18. 12–27	Gen. 27.41 – 28.end 2 Tim. 2. 14–end
Ps. 65; **66** Gen. 29. 1–30 2 Tim. ch. 3 **ct**	G	Eccles. ch. 6 John 18. 28–end	Gen. 29. 1–30 2 Tim. ch. 3 **ct**
Ps. 148 Prov. 8. 1, 22–31 Rev. ch. 4 *Gospel:* Luke 12. 16–31	**SEXAGESIMA** Gen. 3. 9–19 Ps. 83. 1–2, 13–end 2 Cor. 11. 19–31 Luke 8. 4–15 G	Ps. 100; 150 Job 38. 1–21 Col. 1. 15–20	Ps. 148 Prov. 8. 1, 22–31 Rev. ch. 4
Ps. **72**; 75 Gen. 29.31 – 30.24 2 Tim. 4. 1–8	G	Eccles. 7. 1–14 John 19. 1–16	Gen. 29.31 – 30.24 2 Tim. 4. 1–8
Ps. 74 Gen. 31. 1–24 2 Tim. 4. 9–end	G	Eccles. 7. 15–end John 19. 17–30	Gen. 31. 1–24 2 Tim. 4. 9–end
Ps. 119. 81–104 Gen. 31.25 – 32.2 Titus ch. 1	G	Eccles. ch. 8 John 19. 31–end	Gen. 31.25 – 32.2 Titus ch. 1

February 2017

			Sunday Principal Service / Weekday Eucharist	Third Service / Morning Prayer
23	Th	**Polycarp, Bishop of Smyrna, Martyr, c. 155** Com. Martyr *also* Rev. 2. 8–11	*or*	Ecclus. 5. 1–8 *or* James 2. 1–9 Ps. 1 *or* Ps. 34. 1–7 Mark 9. 41–end	Ps. 78. 1–39† Eccles. ch. 9 John 20. 1–10
	Gr				
24	F*			Ecclus. 6. 5–17 *or* James 2. 14–24, 26 Ps. 119. 19–24 *or* Ps. 112 Mark 10. 1–12	Ps. 55 Eccles. 11. 1–8 John 20. 11–18
	G				
25	Sa			Ecclus. 17. 1–15 *or* James 3. 1–10 Ps. 103. 13–18 *or* Ps. 12. 1–7 Mark 10. 13–16	Ps. **76**; 79 Eccles. 11.9 – 12.end John 20. 19–end
	G				
26	S	THE SUNDAY NEXT BEFORE LENT		Exod. 24. 12–end Ps. 2 *or* Ps. 99 2 Pet. 1. 16–end Matt. 17. 1–9	Ps. 72 Exod. 34. 29–end 2 Cor. 4. 3–6
	G				
27 DEL 8	M	**George Herbert, Priest, Poet, 1633** Com. Pastor *esp.* Mal. 2. 5–7 Matt. 11. 25–end *also* Rev. 19. 5–9	*or*	Ecclus. 17. 24–29 *or* James 3. 13–end Ps. 32. 1–8 *or* Ps. 19. 7–end Mark 10. 17–27	Ps. **80**; 82 Jer. ch. 1 John 3. 1–21
	Gw				
28	Tu			Ecclus. 35. 1–12 *or* James 4. 1–10 Ps. 50. 1–6 *or* Ps. 55. 7–9, 24 Mark 10. 28–31	Ps. 87; **89. 1–18** Jer. 2. 1–13 John 3. 22–end
	G				

March 2017

			Sunday Principal Service / Weekday Eucharist	Third Service / Morning Prayer
1	W	**ASH WEDNESDAY**	Joel 2. 1–2, 12–17 *or* Isa. 58. 1–12 Ps. 51. 1–18 2 Cor. 5.20b – 6.10 Matt. 6. 1–6, 16–21 *or* John 8. 1–11	MP: Ps. 38 Dan. 9. 3–6, 17–19 1 Tim. 6. 6–19
	P			
2	Th	**Chad, Bishop of Lichfield, Missionary, 672** Com. Missionary *also* 1 Tim. 6. 11b–16	*or* Deut. 30. 15–end Ps. 1 Luke 9. 22–25	Ps. 77 *alt.* Ps. 90; **92** Jer. 2. 14–32 John 4. 1–26
	Pw			
3	F		Isa. 58. 1–9a Ps. 51. 1–5, 17–18 Matt. 9. 14–15	Ps. **3**; 7 *alt.* Ps. **88**; (95) Jer. 3. 6–22 John 4. 27–42
	P			
4	Sa		Isa. 58. 9b–end Ps. 86. 1–7 Luke 5. 27–32	Ps. 71 *alt.* Ps. 96; **97**; 100 Jer. 4. 1–18 John 4. 43–end
	P			

*Matthias may be celebrated on 24 February instead of 15 May.
**Chad may be celebrated with Cedd on 26 October instead of 2 March.

Second Service Evening Prayer	Calendar and Holy Communion		Morning Prayer	Evening Prayer
Ps. 78. 40–end† Gen. 32. 3–30 Titus ch. 2		G	Eccles. ch. 9 John 20. 1–10	Gen. 32. 3–30 Titus ch. 2 or First EP of Matthias (Ps. 147) Isa. 22. 15–22 Phil. 3.13b – 4.1 R ct
Ps. 69 Gen. 33. 1–17 Titus ch. 3	MATTHIAS THE APOSTLE I Sam. 2. 27–35 Ps. 16. 1–7 Acts 1. 15–end Matt. 1. 25–end	R	(Ps. 15) Jonah 1. 1–9 Acts 2. 37–end	(Ps. 80) I Sam. 16. 1–13a Matt. 7. 15–27
Ps. 81; 84 Gen. ch. 35 Philemon ct		G	Eccles. 11.9 – 12.end John 20. 19–end	Gen. ch. 35 Philemon ct
Ps. 84 Ecclus. 48. 1–10 or 2 Kings 2. 1–12 Matt. 17. [1–8] 9–23	QUINQUAGESIMA Gen. 9. 8–17 Ps. 77. 11–end I Cor. ch. 13 Luke 18. 31–43	G	Ps. 72 Exod. 34. 29–end 2 Cor. 4. 3–6	Ps. 84 Ecclus. 48. 1–10 or 2 Kings 2. 1–12 Matt. 17. [1–8] 9–23
Ps. 85; 86 Gen. 37. 1–11 Gal. ch. 1		G	Jer. ch. 1 John 3. 1–21	Gen. 37. 1–11 Gal. ch. 1
Ps. 89. 19–end Gen. 37. 12–end Gal. 2. 1–10		G	Jer. 2. 1–13 John 3. 22–end	Gen. 37. 12–end Gal. 2. 1–10
EP: Ps. 51 or Ps. 102 (or 102.1–18) Isa. 1. 10–18 Luke 15. 11–end	ASH WEDNESDAY Ash Wed. Collect until 15 April Commination Joel 2. 12–17 Ps. 57 James 4. 1–10 Matt. 6. 16–21	P	Ps. 38 Dan. 9. 3–6, 17–19 I Tim. 6. 6–19	Ps. 51 or Ps. 102 (or 102.1–18) Isa. 1. 10–18 Luke 15. 11–end
Ps. 74 alt. Ps. 94 Gen. ch. 39 Gal. 2. 11–end	Chad, Bishop of Lichfield, Missionary, 672 Com. Bishop or Exod. 24. 12–end Matt. 8. 5–13	Pw	Jer. 2. 14–32 John 4. 1–26	Gen. ch. 39 Gal. 2. 11–end
Ps. 31 alt. Ps. 102 Gen. ch. 40 Gal. 3. 1–14	I Kings 19. 3b–8 Matt. 5.43 – 6.6	P	Jer. 3. 6–22 John 4. 27–42	Gen. ch. 40 Gal. 3. 1–14
Ps. 73 alt. Ps. 104 Gen. 41. 1–24 Gal. 3. 15–22 ct	Isa. 38. 1–6a Mark 6. 45–end	P	Jer. 4. 1–18 John 4. 43–end	Gen. 41. 1–24 Gal. 3. 15–22 ct

March 2017

		Sunday Principal Service Weekday Eucharist	Third Service Morning Prayer
5	S	THE FIRST SUNDAY OF LENT	
		Gen. 2. 15–17; 3. 1–7 Ps. 32 Rom. 5. 12–19 Matt. 4. 1–11	Ps. 119. 1–16 Jer. 18. 1–11 Luke 18. 9–14
	P		
6	M	Lev. 19. 1–2, 11–18 Ps. 19. 7–end Matt. 25. 31–end	Ps. 10; *11* *alt.* Ps. *98*; 99; 101 Jer. 4. 19–end
	P		John 5. 1–18
7	Tu	**Perpetua, Felicity and their Companions, Martyrs at Carthage, 203**	
		Com. Martyr *or* *esp.* Rev. 12. 10–12a *also* Wisd. 3. 1–7	Isa. 55. 10–11 Ps. 34. 4–6, 21–22 Matt. 6. 7–15	Ps. 44 *alt.* Ps. *106*† (*or* 103) Jer. 5. 1–19
	Pr		John 5. 19–29
8	W	**Edward King, Bishop of Lincoln, 1910** Ember Day* *Felix, Bishop, Apostle to the East Angles, 647; Geoffrey Studdert Kennedy, Priest, Poet, 1929* Com. Bishop *or* *also* Heb. 13. 1–8	Jonah ch. 3 Ps. 51. 1–5, 17–18 Luke 11. 29–32	Ps. *6*; 17 *alt.* Ps. 110; *111*; 112 Jer. 5. 20–end
	Pw		John 5. 30–end
9	Th	Esther 14. 1–5, 12–14 *or* Isa. 55. 6–9 Ps. 138 Matt. 7. 7–12	Ps. *42*; 43 *alt.* Ps. 113; *115* Jer. 6. 9–21
	P		John 6. 1–15
10	F	Ember Day*	
		Ezek. 18. 21–28 Ps. 130 Matt. 5. 20–26	Ps. 22 *alt.* Ps. 139 Jer. 6. 22–end
	P		John 6. 16–27
11	Sa	Ember Day*	
		Deut. 26. 16–end Ps. 119. 1–8 Matt. 5. 43–end	Ps. 59; *63* *alt.* Ps. 120; *121*; 122 Jer. 7. 1–20
	P		John 6. 27–40
12	S	THE SECOND SUNDAY OF LENT	
		Gen. 12. 1–4a Ps. 121 Rom. 4. 1–5, 13–17	Ps. 74 Jer. 22. 1–9 Matt. 8. 1–13
	P	John 3. 1–17	
13	M	Dan. 9. 4–10 Ps. 79. 8–9, 12, 14 Luke 6. 36–38	Ps. 26; *32* *alt.* Ps. 123; 124; 125; *126* Jer. 7. 21–end
	P		John 6. 41–51
14	Tu	Isa. 1. 10, 16–20 Ps. 50. 8, 16–end Matt. 23. 1–12	Ps. 50 *alt.* Ps. *132*; 133 Jer. 8. 1–15
	P		John 6. 52–59
15	W	Jer. 18. 18–20 Ps. 31. 4–5, 14–18 Matt. 20. 17–28	Ps. 35 *alt.* Ps. 119. 153–end Jer. 8.18 – 9.11
	P		John 6. 60–end

*For Ember Day provision, see p. 11.

Second Service Evening Prayer		Calendar and Holy Communion	Morning Prayer	Evening Prayer
Ps. 50. 1–15 Deut. 6. 4–9, 16–end Luke 15. 1–10		**THE FIRST SUNDAY IN LENT** Collect (1) Lent 1 (2) Ash Wednesday Ember until the 11th Gen. 3. 1–6 Ps. 91. 1–12 2 Cor. 6. 1–10	Ps. 119. 1–16 Jer. 18. 1–11 Luke 18. 9–14	Ps. 50. 1–15 Deut. 6. 4–9, 16–end Luke 15. 1–10
	P	Matt. 4. 1–11		
Ps. 12; *13*; 14 *alt.* Ps. *105*† (or 103) Gen. 41. 25–45 Gal. 3.23 – 4.7	P	Ezek. 34. 11–16a Matt. 25. 31–end	Jer. 4. 19–end John 5. 1–18	Gen. 41. 25–45 Gal. 3.23 – 4.7
Ps. 46; *49* *alt.* Ps. 107† Gen. 41.46 – 42.5 Gal. 4. 8–20	Pr	**Perpetua, Martyr at Carthage, 203** Com. Martyr *or* Isa. 55. 6–11 Matt. 21. 10–16	Jer. 5. 1–19 John 5. 19–29	Gen. 41.46 – 42.5 Gal. 4. 8–20
Ps. 9; *28* *alt.* Ps. 119. 129–152 Gen. 42. 6–17 Gal. 4.21 – 5.1	P	Ember Day Ember CEG *or* Isa. 58. 1–9a Matt. 12. 38–end	Jer. 5. 20–end John 5. 30–end	Gen. 42. 6–17 Gal. 4.21 – 5.1
Ps. 137; 138; *142* *alt.* Ps. 114; *116*; 117 Gen. 42. 18–28 Gal. 5. 2–15	P	Isa. 58. 9b–end John 8. 31–45	Jer. 6. 9–21 John 6. 1–15	Gen. 42. 18–28 Gal. 5. 2–15
Ps. 54; *55* *alt.* Ps. *130*; 131; 137 Gen. 42. 29–end Gal. 5. 16–end	P	Ember Day Ember CEG *or* Ezek. 18. 20–25 John 5. 2–15	Jer. 6. 22–end John 6. 16–27	Gen. 42. 29–end Gal. 5. 16–end
Ps. 4; 16 *alt.* Ps. 118 Gen. 43. 1–15 Gal. ch. 6 ct	P	Ember Day Ember CEG *or* Ezek. 18. 26–end Matt. 17. 1–9 *or* Luke 4. 16–21 *or* John 10. 1–16	Jer. 7. 1–20 John 6. 27–40	Gen. 43. 1–15 Gal. ch. 6 ct
Ps. 135 (*or* 135. 1–14) Num. 21. 4–9 Luke 14. 27–33	P	**THE SECOND SUNDAY IN LENT** Jer. 17. 5–10 Ps. 25. 13–end 1 Thess. 4. 1–8 Matt. 15. 21–28	Ps. 74 Jer. 22. 1–9 Matt. 8. 1–13	Ps. 135 (*or* 135. 1–14) Num. 21. 4–9 Luke 14. 27–33
Ps. 70; *74* *alt.* Ps. *127*; 128; 129 Gen. 43. 16–end Heb. ch. 1	P	Heb. 2. 1–10 John 8. 21–30	Jer. 7. 21–end John 6. 41–51	Gen. 43. 16–end Heb. ch. 1
Ps. *52*; 53; 54 *alt.* Ps. (134); *135* Gen. 44. 1–17 Heb. 2. 1–9	P	Heb. 2. 11–end Matt. 23. 1–12	Jer. 8. 1–15 John 6. 52–59	Gen. 44. 1–17 Heb. 2. 1–9
Ps. *3*; 51 *alt.* Ps. 136 Gen. 44. 18–end Heb. 2. 10–end	P	Heb. 3. 1–6 Matt. 20. 17–28	Jer. 8.18 – 9.11 John 6. 60–end	Gen. 44. 18–end Heb. 2. 10–end

March 2017

		Sunday Principal Service Weekday Eucharist	Third Service Morning Prayer

16 Th

P

Jer. 17. 5–10
Ps. 1
Luke 16. 19–end

Ps. 34
alt. Ps. *143*; 146
Jer. 9. 12–24
John 7. 1–13

---

17 F

Pw

Patrick, Bishop, Missionary, Patron of Ireland, c. 460
Com. Missionary   *or*
also Ps. 91. 1–4, 13–end
Luke 10. 1–12, 17–20

Gen. 37. 3–4, 12–13, 17–28
Ps. 105. 16–22
Matt. 21. 33–43, 45–46

Ps. 40; *41*
alt. Ps. 142; *144*
Jer. 10. 1–16
John 7. 14–24

---

18 Sa

P

Cyril, Bishop of Jerusalem, Teacher, 386

Mic. 7. 4–15, 18–20
Ps. 103. 1–4, 9–12
Luke 15. 1–3, 11–end

Ps. 3; *25*
alt. Ps. 147
Jer. 10. 17–24
John 7. 25–36

---

19 S

P

THE THIRD SUNDAY OF LENT
(Joseph transferred to 20 March)

Exod. 17. 1–7
Ps. 95
Rom. 5. 1–11
John 4. 5–42

Ps. 46
Amos 7. 10–end
2 Cor. 1. 1–11

---

20 M*

W

JOSEPH OF NAZARETH (transferred from 19 March)**

2 Sam. 7. 4–16
Ps. 89. 27–36
Rom. 4. 13–18
Matt. 1. 18–end

MP: Ps. 25; 147. 1–12
Isa. 11. 1–10
Matt. 13. 54–end

---

21 Tu

Pr

Thomas Cranmer, Archbishop of Canterbury, Reformation Martyr, 1556
Com. Martyr   *or*

Song of the Three 2, 11–20
or Dan. 2. 20–23
Ps. 25. 3–10
Matt. 18. 21–end

Ps. 6; *9*
alt. Ps. *5*; 6; (8)
Jer. 11.18 – 12.6
John 7.53 – 8.11

---

22 W

P

Deut. 4. 1, 5–9
Ps. 147. 13–end
Matt. 5. 17–19

Ps. 38
alt. Ps. 119. 1–32
Jer. 13. 1–11
John 8. 12–30

---

23 Th

P

Jer. 7. 23–28
Ps. 95. 1–2, 6–end
Luke 11. 14–23

Ps. *56*; 57
alt. Ps. 14; *15*; 16
Jer. ch. 14
John 8. 31–47

---

24 F

P

Walter Hilton of Thurgarton, Augustinian Canon, Mystic, 1396; Paul Couturier, Priest, Ecumenist, 1953;
Oscar Romero, Archbishop of San Salvador, Martyr, 1980

Hos. ch. 14
Ps. 81. 6–10, 13, 16
Mark 12. 28–34

Ps. 22
alt. Ps. 17; *19*
Jer. 15. 10–end
John 8. 48–end

---

25 Sa

⅏

THE ANNUNCIATION OF OUR LORD TO THE BLESSED VIRGIN MARY

Isa. 7. 10–14
Ps. 40. 5–11
Heb. 10. 4–10
Luke 1. 26–38

MP: Ps. 111; 113
1 Sam. 2. 1–10
Rom. 5. 12–end

---

*The following readings may replace those provided for Holy Communion on any day (except Joseph of Nazareth and The Annunciation)
during the Third Week of Lent: Exod. 17. 1–7; Ps. 95. 1–2, 6–end; John 4. 5–42.
**Cuthbert may be celebrated on 4 September instead of 20 March.

Second Service Evening Prayer		Calendar and Holy Communion	Morning Prayer	Evening Prayer
Ps. 71 *alt.* Ps. *138*; 140; 141 Gen. 45. 1–15 Heb. 3. 1–6	P	Heb. 3. 7–end John 5. 30–end	Jer. 9. 12–24 John 7. 1–13	Gen. 45. 1–15 Heb. 3. 1–6
Ps. *6*; 38 *alt.* Ps. 145 Gen. 45. 16–end Heb. 3. 7–end	P	Heb. ch. 4 Matt. 21. 33–end	Jer. 10. 1–16 John 7. 14–24	Gen. 45. 16–end Heb. 3. 7–end
Ps. *23*; 27 *alt.* Ps. *148*; 149; 150 Gen. 46. 1–7, 28–end Heb. 4. 1–13 ct	Pr	**Edward, King of the West Saxons, 978** Com. Martyr *or* Heb. ch. 5 Luke 15. 11–end	Jer. 10. 17–24 John 7. 25–36	Gen. 46. 1–7, 28–end Heb. 4. 1–13 ct
Ps. 40 Josh. 1. 1–9 Eph. 6. 10–20 *Gospel:* John 2. 13–22 *or First EP of Joseph* Ps. 132 Hos. 11. 1–9 Luke 2. 41–end	P	**THE THIRD SUNDAY IN LENT** Num. 22. 21–31 Ps. 9. 13–end Eph. 5. 1–14 Luke 11. 14–28	Ps. 46 Amos 7. 10–end 2 Cor. 1. 1–11	Ps. 40 Josh. 1. 1–9 Eph. 6. 10–20
EP: Ps. 1; 112 Gen. 50. 22–end Matt. 2. 13–end	P	To celebrate Joseph, see *Common Worship* provision. Heb. 6. 1–10 Luke 4. 23–30	Jer. 11. 1–17 John 7. 37–52	Gen. 47. 1–27 Heb. 4.14 – 5.10
Ps. 61; 62; *64* *alt.* Ps. *9*; 10† Gen. 47.28 – 48.end Heb. 5.11 – 6.12	Pw	**Benedict, Abbot of Monte Cassino, *c.* 550** Com. Abbot *or* Heb. 6. 11–end Matt. 18. 15–22	Jer. 11.18 – 12.6 John 7.53 – 8.11	Gen. 47.28 – 48.end Heb. 5.11 – 6.12
Ps. 36; *39* *alt.* Ps. *11*; 12; 13 Gen. 49. 1–32 Heb. 6. 13–end	P	Heb. 7. 1–10 Matt. 15. 1–20	Jer. 13. 1–11 John 8. 12–30	Gen. 49. 1–32 Heb. 6. 13–end
Ps. *59*; 60 *alt.* Ps. 18† Gen. 49.33 – 50.end Heb. 7. 1–10	P	Heb. 7. 11–25 John 6. 26–35	Jer. ch. 14 John 8. 31–47	Gen. 49.33 – 50.end Heb. 7. 1–10
First EP of The Annunciation Ps. 85 Wisd. 9. 1–12 *or* Gen. 3. 8–15 Gal. 4. 1–5 ℣ ct	P	Heb. 7. 26–end John 4. 5–26	Jer. 15. 10–end John 8. 48–end	*First EP of The Annunciation* Ps. 85 Wisd. 9. 1–12 *or* Gen. 3. 8–15 Gal. 4. 1–5 ℣ ct
EP: Ps. 131; 146 Isa. 52. 1–12 Heb. 2. 5–end	℣	**THE ANNUNCIATION OF THE BLESSED VIRGIN MARY** Isa. 7. 10–14 [15] Ps. 113 Rom. 5. 12–19 Luke 1. 26–38	Ps. 111 1 Sam. 2. 1–10 Heb. 10. 4–10	Ps. 131; 146 Isa. 52. 1–12 Heb. 2. 5–end

March 2017

		Sunday Principal Service Weekday Eucharist	Third Service Morning Prayer
26	S	THE FOURTH SUNDAY OF LENT (Mothering Sunday)	
		I Sam. 16. 1–13 Ps. 23 Eph. 5. 8–14 John ch. 9	Ps. 19 Isa. 43. 1–7 Eph. 2. 8–14
		or, for Mothering Sunday:	
		Exod. 2. 1–10 *or* I Sam. 1. 20–end Ps. 34. 11–20 *or* Ps. 127. 1–4 2 Cor. 1. 3–7 *or* Col. 3. 12–17 Luke 2. 33–35 *or* John 19. 25b–27	
	P		
27	M*	Isa. 65. 17–21 Ps. 30. 1–5, 8, 11–end John 4. 43–end	Ps. 70; **77** *alt.* Ps. 27; **30** Jer. 17. 5–18 John 9. 18–end
	P		
28	Tu	Ezek. 47. 1–9, 12 Ps. 46. 1–8 John 5. 1–3, 5–16	Ps. 54; **79** *alt.* Ps. 32; **36** Jer. 18. 1–12 John 10. 1–10
	P		
29	W	Isa. 49. 8–15 Ps. 145. 8–18 John 5. 17–30	Ps. **63**; 90 *alt.* Ps. 34 Jer. 18. 13–end John 10. 11–21
	P		
30	Th	Exod. 32. 7–14 Ps. 106. 19–23 John 5. 31–end	Ps. 53; **86** *alt.* Ps. 37† Jer. 19. 1–13 John 10. 22–end
	P		
31	F	*John Donne, Priest, Poet, 1631*	
		Wisd. 2. 1, 12–22 *or* Jer. 26. 8–11 Ps. 34. 15–end John 7. 1–2, 10, 25–30	Ps. 102 *alt.* Ps. 31 Jer. 19.14 – 20.6 John 11. 1–16
	P		

April 2017

		Sunday Principal Service Weekday Eucharist	Third Service Morning Prayer
1	Sa	*Frederick Denison Maurice, Priest, Teacher, 1872*	
		Jer. 11. 18–20 Ps. 7. 1–2, 8–10 John 7. 40–52	Ps. 32 *alt.* Ps. 41; **42**; 43 Jer. 20. 7–end John 11. 17–27
	P		
2	S	THE FIFTH SUNDAY OF LENT **(Passiontide begins)**	
		Ezek. 37. 1–14 Ps. 130 Rom. 8. 6–11 John 11. 1–45	Ps. 86 Jer. 31. 27–37 John 12. 20–33
	P		
3	M**	Susanna 1–9, 15–17, 19–30, 33–62 (*or* 41b–62) *or* Josh. 2. 1–14 Ps. 23 John 8. 1–11	Ps. **73**; 121 *alt.* Ps. 44 Jer. 21. 1–10 John 11. 28–44
	P		

*The following readings may replace those provided for Holy Communion on any day during the Fourth Week of Lent: Mic. 7. 7–9; Ps. 27. 1, 9–10, 16–17; John ch. 9.

**The following readings may replace those provided for Holy Communion on any day during the Fifth Week of Lent: 2 Kings 4. 18–21, 32–37; Ps. 17. 1–8, 16; John 11. 1–45.

Second Service Evening Prayer	Calendar and Holy Communion	Morning Prayer	Evening Prayer
	THE FOURTH SUNDAY IN LENT To celebrate Mothering Sunday, see *Common Worship* provision.		
Ps. 31. 1–16 (*or* 31. 1–8) Mic. ch. 7 *or* Prayer of Manasseh James ch. 5 *Gospel:* John 3. 14–21 *If the Principal Service readings* *for The Fourth Sunday of Lent* *are displaced by Mothering* *Sunday provisions, they may* *be used at the Second Service.*	Exod. 16. 2–7a Ps. 122 Gal. 4. 21–end *or* Heb. 12. 22–24 John 6. 1–14	Ps. 19 Isa. 43. 1–7 Eph. 2. 8–14	Ps. 31. 1–16 (*or* 31. 1–8) Mic. ch. 7 *or* Prayer of Manasseh James ch. 5
	P		
Ps. **25**; 28 *alt.* Ps. 26; **28**; 29 Exod. 2. 11–22 Heb. 9. 1–14	Heb. 11. 1–6 John 2. 13–end **P**	Jer. 17. 5–18 John 9. 18–end	Exod. 2. 11–22 Heb. 9. 1–14
Ps. **80**; 82 *alt.* Ps. 33 Exod. 2.23 – 3.20 Heb. 9. 15–end	Heb. 11. 13–16a John 7. 14–24 **P**	Jer. 18. 1–12 John 10. 1–10	Exod. 2.23 – 3.20 Heb. 9. 15–end
Ps. 52; **91** *alt.* Ps. 119. 33–56 Exod. 4. 1–23 Heb. 10. 1–18	Heb. 12. 1–11 John 9. 1–17 **P**	Jer. 18. 13–end John 10. 11–21	Exod. 4. 1–23 Heb. 10. 1–18
Ps. 94 *alt.* Ps. 39; **40** Exod. 4.27 – 6.1 Heb. 10. 19–25	Heb. 12. 12–17 John 5. 17–27 **P**	Jer. 19. 1–13 John 10. 22–end	Exod. 4.27 – 6.1 Heb. 10. 19–25
Ps. 13; **16** *alt.* Ps. 35 Exod. 6. 2–13 Heb. 10. 26–end	Heb. 12. 22–end John 11. 33–46 **P**	Jer. 19.14 – 20.6 John 11. 1–16	Exod. 6. 2–13 Heb. 10. 26–end
Ps. **140**; 141; 142 *alt.* Ps. 45; **46** Exod. 7. 8–end Heb. 11. 1–16 **ct**	Heb. 13. 7–21 John 8. 12–20 **P**	Jer. 20. 7–end John 11. 17–27	Exod. 7. 8–end Heb. 11. 1–16 **ct**
	THE FIFTH SUNDAY IN LENT		
Ps. 30 Lam. 3. 19–33 Matt. 20. 17–end	Exod. 24. 4–8 Ps. 143 Heb. 9. 11–15 John 8. 46–end **P**	Ps. 86 Jer. 31. 27–37 John 12. 20–33	Ps. 30 Lam. 3. 19–33 Matt. 20. 17–end
Ps. **26**; 27 *alt.* Ps. **47**; 49 Exod. 8. 1–19 Heb. 11. 17–31	**Richard, Bishop of Chichester, 1253** Com. Bishop *or* Col. 1. 13–23a John 7. 1–13 **Pw**	Jer. 21. 1–10 John 11. 28–44	Exod. 8. 1–19 Heb. 11. 17–31

April 2017

			Sunday Principal Service Weekday Eucharist	Third Service Morning Prayer
4	Tu P		Num. 21. 4–9 Ps. 102. 1–3, 16–23 John 8. 21–30	Ps. *35*; 123 *alt.* Ps. *48*; 52 Jer. 22. 1–5, 13–19 John 11. 45–end
5	W P		Dan. 3. 14–20, 24–25, 28 *Canticle:* Bless the Lord John 8. 31–42	Ps. *55*; 124 *alt.* Ps. 119. 57–80 Jer. 22.20 – 23.8 John 12. 1–11
6	Th P		Gen. 17. 3–9 Ps. 105. 4–9 John 8. 51–end	Ps. *40*; 125 *alt.* Ps. 56; *57*; (63†) Jer. 23. 9–32 John 12. 12–19
7	F P		Jer. 20. 10–13 Ps. 18. 1–6 John 10. 31–end	Ps. *22*; 126 *alt.* Ps. *51*; 54 Jer. ch. 24 John 12. 20–36a
8	Sa P		Ezek. 37. 21–end *Canticle:* Jer. 31. 10–13 *or* Ps. 121 John 11. 45–end	Ps. *23*; 127 *alt.* Ps. 68 Jer. 25. 1–14 John 12. 36b–end
9	S R	PALM SUNDAY *Liturgy of the Palms* Matt. 21. 1–11 Ps. 118. 1–2, 19–end (*or* 118. 19–24)	*Liturgy of the Passion* Isa. 50. 4–9a Ps. 31. 9–16 (*or* 31. 9–18) Phil. 2. 5–11 Matt. 26.14 – 27.end *or* Matt. 27. 11–54	Ps. 61; 62 Zech. 9. 9–12 Luke 16. 19–end
10	M R	MONDAY OF HOLY WEEK	Isa. 42. 1–9 Ps. 36. 5–11 Heb. 9. 11–15 John 12. 1–11	*MP:* Ps. 41 Lam. 1. 1–12a Luke 22. 1–23
11	Tu R	TUESDAY OF HOLY WEEK	Isa. 49. 1–7 Ps. 71. 1–8 [9–14] I Cor. 1. 18–31 John 12. 20–36	*MP:* Ps. 27 Lam. 3. 1–18 Luke 22. [24–38] 39–53
12	W R	WEDNESDAY OF HOLY WEEK	Isa. 50. 4–9a Ps. 70 Heb. 12. 1–3 John 13. 21–32	*MP:* Ps. 102 (*or* 102. 1–8) Wisd. 1.16 – 2.1, 12–22 *or* Jer. 11. 18–20 Luke 22. 54–end
13	Th W (HC) R	**MAUNDY THURSDAY**	Exod. 12. 1–4 [5–10], 11–14 Ps. 116. 1, 10–end (*or* 116. 9–end) I Cor. 11. 23–26 John 13. 1–17, 31b–35	*MP:* Ps. 42; 43 Lev. 16. 2–24 Luke 23. 1–25
14	F R	**GOOD FRIDAY**	Isa. 52.13 – 53.end Ps. 22 (*or* 22. 1–11 *or* 22. 1–21) Heb. 10. 16–25 *or* Heb. 10. 14–16; 5. 7–9 John 18.1 – 19.end	*MP:* Ps. 69 Gen. 22. 1–18 *A part of* John 18 – 19 *if not read at the* *Principal Service* *or* Heb. 10. 1–10

Second Service Evening Prayer		Calendar and Holy Communion	Morning Prayer	Evening Prayer
Ps. *61*; 64 *alt.* Ps. 50 Exod. 8. 20–end Heb. 11.32 – 12.2	**Pw**	**Ambrose, Bishop of Milan, 397** Com. Doctor *or* Col. 2. 8–12 John 7. 32–39	Jer. 22. 1–5, 13–19 John 11. 45–end	Exod. 8. 20–end Heb. 11.32 – 12.2
Ps. 56; *62* *alt.* Ps. *59*; 60 (67) Exod. 9. 1–12 Heb. 12. 3–13	**P**	Col. 2. 13–19 John 7. 40–end	Jer. 22.20 – 23.8 John 12. 1–11	Exod. 9. 1–12 Heb. 12. 3–13
Ps. 42; *43* *alt.* Ps. 61; *62*; 64 Exod. 9. 13–end Heb. 12. 14–end	**P**	Col. 3. 8–11 John 10. 22–38	Jer. 23. 9–32 John 12. 12–19	Exod. 9. 13–end Heb. 12. 14–end
Ps. 31 *alt.* Ps. 38 Exod. ch. 10 Heb. 13. 1–16	**P**	Col. 3. 12–17 John 11. 47–54	Jer. ch. 24 John 12. 20–36a	Exod. ch. 10 Heb. 13. 1–16
Ps. 128; 129; *130* *alt.* Ps. 65; *66* Exod. ch. 11 Heb. 13. 17–end **ct**	**P**	Col. 4. 2–6 John 6. 53–end	Jer. 25. 1–14 John 12. 36b–end	Exod. ch. 11 Heb. 13. 17–end **ct**
Ps. 80 Isa. 5. 1–7 Matt. 21. 33–end	**R**	**THE SUNDAY NEXT BEFORE EASTER (PALM SUNDAY)** Zech. 9. 9–12 Ps. 73. 22–end Phil. 2. 5–11 Passion acc. to Matthew Matt. 27. 1–54 *or* Matt. 26.1 – 27.61 *or* Matt. 21. 1–13	Ps. 61; 62 Isa. 42. 1–9 Luke 16. 19–end	Ps. 80 Isa. 5. 1–7 Matt. 21. 33–end
EP: Ps. 25 Lam. 2. 8–19 Col. 1. 18–23	**R**	**MONDAY IN HOLY WEEK** Isa. 63. 1–19 Ps. 55. 1–8 Gal. 6. 1–11 Mark ch. 14	Ps. 41 Lam. 1. 1–12a John 12. 1–11	Ps. 25 Lam. 2. 8–19 Col. 1. 18–23
EP: Ps. 55. 13–24 Lam. 3. 40–51 Gal. 6. 11–end	**R**	**TUESDAY IN HOLY WEEK** Isa. 50. 5–11 Ps. 13 Rom. 5. 6–19 Mark 15. 1–39	Ps. 27 Lam. 3. 1–18 John 12. 20–36	Ps. 55. 13–24 Lam. 3. 40–51 Gal. 6. 11–end
EP: Ps. 88 Isa. 63. 1–9 Rev. 14.18 – 15.4	**R**	**WEDNESDAY IN HOLY WEEK** Isa. 49. 1–9a Ps. 54 Heb. 9. 16–end Luke ch. 22	Ps. 102 (*or* 102. 1–8) Wisd. 1.16 – 2.1, 12–22 *or* Jer. 11. 18–20 John 13. 21–32	Ps. 88 Isa. 63. 1–9 Rev. 14.18 – 15.4
EP: Ps. 39 Exod. ch. 11 Eph. 2. 11–18	**W (HC) R**	**MAUNDY THURSDAY** Exod. 12. 1–11 Ps. 43 1 Cor. 11. 17–end Luke 23. 1–49	Ps. 42; 43 Lev. 16. 2–24 John 13. 1–17, 31b–35	Ps. 39 Exod. ch. 11 Eph. 2. 11–18
EP: Ps. 130; 143 Lam. 5. 15–end John 19. 38–end *or* Col. 1. 18–23	**R**	**GOOD FRIDAY** Alt. Collect Passion acc. to John Alt. Gospel, if Passion is read Num. 21. 4–9 Ps. 140. 1–9 Heb. 10. 1–25 John 19. 1–37 *or* John 19. 38–end	Ps. 69 Gen. 22. 1–18 John ch. 18	Ps. 130; 143 Lam. 5. 15–end John 19. 38–end

April 2017

			Sunday Principal Service Weekday Eucharist	Third Service Morning Prayer
15	Sa	**EASTER EVE** *These readings are for use at services other than the Easter Vigil.*	Job 14. 1–14 *or* Lam. 3. 1–9, 19–24 Ps. 31. 1–4, 15–16 (*or* 31. 1–5) 1 Pet. 4. 1–8 Matt. 27. 57–end *or* John 19. 38–end	Ps. 142 Hos. 6. 1–6 John 2. 18–22
16	S	**EASTER DAY** *The following readings and psalms (or canticles) are provided for use at the Easter Vigil. A minimum of three Old Testament readings should be chosen. The reading from* Exodus ch. 14 *should always be used.*	Gen. 1.1 – 2.4a & Ps. 136. 1–9, 23–end Gen. 7. 1–5, 11–18; 8. 6–18; 9. 8–13 & Ps. 46 Gen. 22. 1–18 & Ps. 16 Exod. 14. 10–end; 15. 20–21 & *Canticle:* Exod. 15. 1b–13, 17–18 Isa. 55. 1–11 & *Canticle:* Isa. 12. 2–end Baruch 3.9–15, 32 – 4.4 & Ps. 19 *or* Prov. 8. 1–8, 19–21; 9. 4b–6 & Ps. 19 Ezek. 36. 24–28 & Ps. 42; 43 Ezek. 37. 1–14 & Ps. 143 Zeph. 3. 14–end & Ps. 98 Rom. 6. 3–11 & Ps. 114 Matt. 28. 1–10	
		Easter Day Services *The reading from Acts must be used as either the first or second reading at the Principal Service.*	Acts 10. 34–43 *or* Jer. 31. 1–6 Ps. 118. 1–2, 14–24 (*or* 118. 14–24) Col. 3. 1–4 *or* Acts 10. 34–43 John 20. 1–18 *or* Matt. 28. 1–10	MP: Ps. 114; 117 Exod. 14.10–18, 26 – 15.2 Rev. 15. 2–4
	☽			
17	M	**MONDAY OF EASTER WEEK**	Acts 2. 14, 22–32 Ps. 16. 1–2, 6–end Matt. 28. 8–15	Ps. *111*; 117; 146 Song of Sol. 1.9 – 2.7 Mark 16. 1–8
	W			
18	Tu	**TUESDAY OF EASTER WEEK**	Acts 2. 36–41 Ps. 33. 4–5, 18–end John 20. 11–18	Ps. *112*; 147. 1–12 Song of Sol. 2. 8–end Luke 24. 1–12
	W			
19	W	**WEDNESDAY OF EASTER WEEK**	Acts 3. 1–10 Ps. 105. 1–9 Luke 24. 13–35	Ps. *113*; 147. 13–end Song of Sol. ch. 3 Matt. 28. 16–end
	W			
20	Th	**THURSDAY OF EASTER WEEK**	Acts 3. 11–end Ps. 8 Luke 24. 35–48	Ps. *114*; 148 Song of Sol. 5.2 – 6.3 Luke 7. 11–17
	W			
21	F	**FRIDAY OF EASTER WEEK**	Acts 4. 1–12 Ps. 118. 1–4, 22–26 John 21. 1–14	Ps. *115*; 149 Song of Sol. 7.10 – 8.4 Luke 8. 41–end
	W			
22	Sa	**SATURDAY OF EASTER WEEK**	Acts 4. 13–21 Ps. 118. 1–4, 14–21 Mark 16. 9–15	Ps. *116*; 150 Song of Sol. 8. 5–7 John 11. 17–44
	W			

Second Service Evening Prayer		Calendar and Holy Communion	Morning Prayer	Evening Prayer
Ps. 116 Job 19. 21–27 1 John 5. 5–12		**EASTER EVE** Job 14. 1–14 1 Pet. 3. 17–22 Matt. 27. 57–end	Ps. 142 Hos. 6. 1–6 John 2. 18–22	Ps. 116 Job 19. 21–27 1 John 5. 5–12
		EASTER DAY Exod. 12. 21–28 Ps. 111 Col. 3. 1–7 John 20. 1–10	Ps. 114; 117 Exod. 14.10–18, 26 – 15.2 Rev. 15. 2–4	Ps. 105 or Ps. 66. 1–11 Song of Sol. 3. 2–5; 8. 6–7 John 20. 11–18 or Rev. 1. 12–18
EP: Ps. 105 or Ps. 66. 1–11 Song of Sol. 3. 2–5; 8. 6–7 or Rev. 1. 12–18 John 20. 11–18 *if not used at the Principal Service*	℣			
Ps. 135 Exod. 12. 1–14 1 Cor. 15. 1–11	W	**MONDAY IN EASTER WEEK** Hos. 6. 1–6 Easter Anthems Acts 10. 34–43 Luke 24. 13–35	Song of Sol. 1.9 – 2.7 Mark 16. 1–8	Exod. 12. 1–14 1 Cor. 15. 1–11
Ps. 136 Exod. 12. 14–36 1 Cor. 15. 12–19	W	**TUESDAY IN EASTER WEEK** 1 Kings 17. 17–end Ps. 16. 9–end Acts 13. 26–41 Luke 24. 36b–48	Song of Sol. 2. 8–end Luke 24. 1–12	Exod. 12. 14–36 1 Cor. 15. 12–19
Ps. 105 Exod. 12. 37–end 1 Cor. 15. 20–28	W	Isa. 42. 10–16 Ps. 111 Acts 3. 12–18 John 20. 11–18	Song of Sol. ch. 3 Matt. 28. 16–end	Exod. 12. 37–end 1 Cor. 15. 20–28
Ps. 106 Exod. 13. 1–16 1 Cor. 15. 29–34	W	Isa. 43. 16–21 Ps. 113 Acts 8. 26–end John 21. 1–14	Song of Sol. 5.2 – 6.3 Luke 7. 11–17	Exod. 13. 1–16 1 Cor. 15. 29–34
Ps. 107 Exod. 13.17 – 14.14 1 Cor. 15. 35–50	W	Ezek. 37. 1–14 Ps. 116. 1–9 1 Pet. 3. 18–end Matt. 28. 16–end	Song of Sol. 7.10 – 8.4 Luke 8. 41–end	Exod. 13.17 – 14.14 1 Cor. 15. 35–50
Ps. 145 Exod. 14. 15–end 1 Cor. 15. 51–end ct	W	Zech. 8. 1–8 Ps. 118. 14–21 1 Pet. 2. 1–10 John 20. 24–end	Song of Sol. 8. 5–7 John 11. 17–44	Exod. 14. 15–end 1 Cor. 15. 51–end ct

April 2017

		Sunday Principal Service Weekday Eucharist	Third Service Morning Prayer
23	S	THE SECOND SUNDAY OF EASTER (George transferred to the 24th) *The reading from Acts must be used as either the first or second reading at the Principal Service.*	Acts 2. 14a, 22–32 [or Exod. 14. 10–end; 15. 20–21] Ps. 16 1 Pet. 1. 3–9 John 20. 19–end	Ps. 81. 1–10 Exod. 12. 1–17 1 Cor. 5. 6b–8
	W			
24	M	GEORGE, MARTYR, PATRON OF ENGLAND, c. 304 (transferred from the 23rd)		
			1 Macc. 2. 59–64 or Rev. 12. 7–12 Ps. 126 2 Tim. 2. 3–13 John 15. 18–21	MP: Ps. 5; 146 Josh. 1. 1–9 Eph. 6. 10–20
	R			
25	Tu	MARK THE EVANGELIST	Prov. 15. 28–end or Acts 15. 35–end Ps. 119. 9–16 Eph. 4. 7–16 Mark 13. 5–13	MP: Ps. 37. 23–end; 148 Isa. 62. 6–10 or Ecclus. 51. 13–end Acts 12.25 – 13.13
	R			
26	W		Acts 5. 17–26 Ps. 34. 1–8 John 3. 16–21	Ps. 16; *30* *alt.* Ps. 119. 1–32 Deut. 3. 18–end John 20. 19–end
	W			
27	Th	*Christina Rossetti, Poet, 1894*	Acts 5. 27–33 Ps. 34. 1, 15–end John 3. 31–end	Ps. *28*; 29 *alt.* Ps. 14; *15*; 16 Deut. 4. 1–14 John 21. 1–14
	W			
28	F	*Peter Chanel, Missionary in the South Pacific, Martyr, 1841*	Acts 5. 34–42 Ps. 27. 1–5, 16–17 John 6. 1–15	Ps. 57; *61* *alt.* Ps. 17; *19* Deut. 4. 15–31 John 21. 15–19
	W			
29	Sa	**Catherine of Siena, Teacher, 1380** Com. Teacher *or* *also* Prov. 8. 1, 6–11 John 17. 12–end	Acts 6. 1–7 Ps. 33. 1–5, 18–19 John 6. 16–21	Ps. 63; *84* *alt.* Ps. 20; 21; *23* Deut. 4. 32–40 John 21. 20–end
	W			
30	S	THE THIRD SUNDAY OF EASTER *The reading from Acts must be used as either the first or second reading at the Principal Service.*	Acts 2. 14a, 36–41 [or Zeph. 3. 14–end] Ps. 116. 1–3, 10–end (or 116. 1–7) 1 Pet. 1. 17–23 Luke 24. 13–35	Ps. 23 Isa. 40. 1–11 1 Pet. 5. 1–11
	W			

May 2017

		Sunday Principal Service Weekday Eucharist	Third Service Morning Prayer
1	M	PHILIP AND JAMES, APOSTLES	Isa. 30. 15–21 Ps. 119. 1–8 Eph. 1. 3–10 John 14. 1–14	MP: Ps. 139; 146 Prov. 4. 10–18 James 1. 1–12
	R			

Second Service Evening Prayer	Calendar and Holy Communion	Morning Prayer	Evening Prayer
	THE FIRST SUNDAY AFTER EASTER		
Ps. 30. 1–5 Dan. 6. [1–5] 6–23 Mark 15.46 – 16.8 *or First EP of George* Ps. 111; 116 Jer. 15. 15–end Heb. 11.32 – 12.2 **R ct**	Ezek. 37. 1–10 Ps. 81. 1–4 1 John 5. 4–12 John 20. 19–23 **W**	Ps. 81. 1–10 Exod. 12. 1–17 1 Cor. 5. 6b–8	Ps. 30. 1–5 Dan. 6. [1–5] 6–23 Mark 15.46 – 16.8
	George, Martyr, Patron of England, c. 304 To celebrate George, see *Common Worship* provision. *Also* Com. Martyr **Wr**	Deut. 1. 3–18 John 20. 1–10	Exod. 15. 1–21 Col. 1. 1–14 *or First EP of Mark* (Ps. 19) Isa. 52. 7–10 Mark 1. 1–15 **R ct**
EP: Ps. 3; 11 Isa. 43. 1–7 John 15. 1–8			
EP: Ps. 45 Ezek. 1. 4–14 2 Tim. 4. 1–11	**MARK THE EVANGELIST** Prov. 15. 28–end Ps. 119. 9–16 Eph. 4. 7–16 John 15. 1–11 **R**	(Ps. 37. 23–end; 148) Isa. 62. 6–10 *or* Ecclus. 51. 13–end Acts 12.25 – 13.13	(Ps. 45) Ezek. 1. 4–14 2 Tim. 4. 1–11
Ps. 33 *alt.* Ps. *11*; 12; 13 Exod. 16. 11–end Col. 2. 1–15 **W**		Deut. 3. 18–end John 20. 19–end	Exod. 16. 11–end Col. 2. 1–15
Ps. 34 *alt.* Ps. 18† Exod. ch. 17 Col. 2.16 – 3.11 **W**		Deut. 4. 1–14 John 21. 1–14	Exod. ch. 17 Col. 2.16 – 3.11
Ps. 118 *alt.* Ps. 22 Exod. 18. 1–12 Col. 3.12 – 4.1 **W**		Deut. 4. 15–31 John 21. 15–19	Exod. 18. 1–12 Col. 3.12 – 4.1
Ps. 66 *alt.* Ps. *24*; 25 Exod. 18. 13–end Col. 4. 2–end **ct**		Deut. 4. 32–40 John 21. 20–end	Exod. 18. 13–end Col. 4. 2–end **ct**
	THE SECOND SUNDAY AFTER EASTER		
Ps. 48 Hag. 1.13 – 2.9 1 Cor. 3. 10–17 *Gospel:* John 2. 13–22 *or First EP of Philip and James* Ps. 25 Isa. 40. 27–end John 12. 20–26 **R ct**	Ezek. 34. 11–16a Ps. 23 1 Pet. 2. 19–end John 10. 11–16 **W**	Ps. 23 Isa. 40. 1–11 1 Pet. 5. 1–11	Ps. 48 Hag. 1.13 – 2.9 1 Cor. 3. 10–17 *or First EP of Philip and James* Ps. 119. 1–8 Isa. 40. 27–end John 12. 20–26 **R ct**
EP: Ps. 149 Job 23. 1–12 John 1. 43–end	**PHILIP AND JAMES, APOSTLES** Prov. 4. 10–18 Ps. 25. 1–9 James 1. [1] 2–12 John 14. 1–14 **R**	(Ps. 139; 146) Isa. 30. 1–5 John 12. 20–26	(Ps. 149) Job 23. 1–12 John 1. 43–end

May 2017

			Sunday Principal Service Weekday Eucharist	Third Service Morning Prayer

2 Tu — **Athanasius, Bishop of Alexandria, Teacher, 373**
Com. Teacher
also Ecclus. 4. 20–28
Matt. 10. 24–27

or Acts 7.51 – 8.1a
Ps. 31. 1–5, 16
John 6. 30–35

Ps. **98**; 99; 100
alt. Ps. 32; **36**
Deut. 5. 22–end
Eph. 1. 15–end

W

---

3 W

Acts 8. 1b–8
Ps. 66. 1–6
John 6. 35–40

Ps. 105
alt. Ps. 34
Deut. ch. 6
Eph. 2. 1–10

W

---

4 Th — **English Saints and Martyrs of the Reformation Era**
Isa. 43. 1–7
or Ecclus. 2. 10–17
Ps. 87
2 Cor. 4. 5–12
John 12. 20–26

or Acts 8. 26–end
Ps. 66. 7–8, 14–end
John 6. 44–51

Ps. 136
alt. Ps. 37†
Deut. 7. 1–11
Eph. 2. 11–end

W

---

5 F

Acts 9. 1–20
Ps. 117
John 6. 52–59

Ps. 107
alt. Ps. 31
Deut. 7. 12–end
Eph. 3. 1–13

W

---

6 Sa

Acts 9. 31–42
Ps. 116. 10–15
John 6. 60–69

Ps. 108; **110**; 111
alt. Ps. 41; **42**; 43
Deut. ch. 8
Eph. 3. 14–end

W

---

7 S — **THE FOURTH SUNDAY OF EASTER**
The reading from Acts must be used as either the first or second reading at the Principal Service.

Acts 2. 42–end
[or Gen. ch. 7]
Ps. 23
1 Pet. 2. 19–end
John 10. 1–10

Ps. 106. 6–24
Neh. 9. 6–15
1 Cor. 10. 1–13

W

---

8 M — **Julian of Norwich, Spiritual Writer, c. 1417**
Com. Religious
also 1 Cor. 13. 8–end
Matt. 5. 13–16

or Acts 11. 1–18
Ps. 42. 1–2; 43. 1–4
John 10. 1–10 (*or* 11–18)

Ps. 103
alt. Ps. 44
Deut. 9. 1–21
Eph. 4. 1–16

W

---

9 Tu

Acts 11. 19–26
Ps. 87
John 10. 22–30

Ps. 139
alt. **48**; 52
Deut. 9.23 – 10.5
Eph. 4. 17–end

W

---

10 W

Acts 12.24 – 13.5
Ps. 67
John 12. 44–end

Ps. 135
alt. Ps. 119. 57–80
Deut. 10. 12–end
Eph. 5. 1–14

W

---

11 Th

Acts 13. 13–25
Ps. 89. 1–2, 20–26
John 13. 16–20

Ps. 118
alt. 56; **57**; (63†)
Deut. 11. 8–end
Eph. 5. 15–end

W

---

12 F — *Gregory Dix, Priest, Monk, Scholar, 1952*

Acts 13. 26–33
Ps. 2
John 14. 1–6

Ps. 33
alt. Ps. **51**; 54
Deut. 12. 1–14
Eph. 6. 1–9

W

---

13 Sa

Acts 13. 44–end
Ps. 98. 1–5
John 14. 7–14

Ps. 34
alt. Ps. 68
Deut. 15. 1–18
Eph. 6. 10–end

W

Second Service Evening Prayer		Calendar and Holy Communion	Morning Prayer	Evening Prayer
Ps. 71 *alt.* Ps. 33 Exod. 20. 1–21 Luke 1. 26–38	W		Deut. 5. 22–end Eph. 1. 15–end	Exod. 20. 1–21 Luke 1. 26–38
Ps. 67; **72** *alt.* Ps. 119. 33–56 Exod. ch. 24 Luke 1. 39–56	Wr	**The Invention of the Cross**	Deut. ch. 6 Eph. 2. 1–10	Exod. ch. 24 Luke 1. 39–56
Ps. 73 *alt.* Ps. 39; **40** Exod. 25. 1–22 Luke 1. 57–end	W		Deut. 7. 1–11 Eph. 2. 11–end	Exod. 25. 1–22 Luke 1. 57–end
Ps. 77 *alt.* Ps. 35 Exod. 28. 1–4a, 29–38 Luke 2. 1–20	W		Deut. 7. 12–end Eph. 3. 1–13	Exod. 28. 1–4a, 29–38 Luke 2. 1–20
Ps. 23; **27** *alt.* Ps. 45; **46** Exod. 29. 1–9 Luke 2. 21–40 ct	W	**John the Evangelist, ante Portam Latinam** CEG of 27 December	Deut. ch. 8 Eph. 3. 14–end	Exod. 29. 1–9 Luke 2. 21–40 ct
Ps. 29. 1–10 Ezra 3. 1–13 Eph. 2. 11–end *Gospel:* Luke 19. 37–end	W	THE THIRD SUNDAY AFTER EASTER Gen. 45. 3–10 Ps. 57 1 Pet. 2. 11–17 John 16. 16–22	Ps. 106. 6–24 Neh. 9. 6–15 1 Cor. 10. 1–13	Ps. 29. 1–10 Ezra 3. 1–13 Eph. 2. 11–end
Ps. 112; 113; **114** *alt.* Ps. **47**; 49 Exod. 32. 1–14 Luke 2. 41–end	W		Deut. 9. 1–21 Eph. 4. 1–16	Exod. 32. 1–14 Luke 2. 41–end
Ps. 115; **116** *alt.* Ps. 50 Exod. 32. 15–34 Luke 3. 1–14	W		Deut. 9.23 – 10.5 Eph. 4. 17–end	Exod. 32. 15–34 Luke 3. 1–14
Ps. **47**; 48 *alt.* Ps. **59**; 60 (67) Exod. ch. 33 Luke 3. 15–22	W		Deut. 10. 12–end Eph. 5. 1–14	Exod. ch. 33 Luke 3. 15–22
Ps. 81; **85** *alt.* Ps. 61; **62**; 64 Exod. 34. 1–10, 27–end Luke 4. 1–13	W		Deut. 11. 8–end Eph. 5. 15–end	Exod. 34. 1–10, 27–end Luke 4. 1–13
Ps. **36**; 40 *alt.* Ps. 38 Exod. 35.20 – 36.7 Luke 4. 14–30	W		Deut. 12. 1–14 Eph. 6. 1–9	Exod. 35.20 – 36.7 Luke 4. 14–30
Ps. **84**; 86 *alt.* Ps. 65; **66** Exod. 40. 17–end Luke 4. 31–37 ct	W		Deut. 15. 1–18 Eph. 6. 10–end	Exod. 40. 17–end Luke 4. 31–37 ct

May 2017

			Sunday Principal Service **Weekday Eucharist**	**Third Service** **Morning Prayer**

14 S — THE FIFTH SUNDAY OF EASTER
(Matthias transferred to the 15th)
The reading from Acts must be used as either the first or second reading at the Principal Service.

Acts 7. 55–end
[or Gen. 8. 1–19]
Ps. 31. 1–5, 15–16 (or 31. 1–5)
I Pet. 2. 2–10
John 14. 1–14

Ps. 30
Ezek. 37. 1–12
John 5. 19–29

W

15 M — MATTHIAS THE APOSTLE (transferred from the 14th)*
The reading from Acts must be used as either the first or second reading at the Eucharist.

Isa. 22. 15–end
or Acts 1. 15–end
Ps. 15
Acts 1. 15–end
or I Cor. 4. 1–7
John 15. 9–17

MP: Ps. 16; 147. 1–12
I Sam. 2. 27–35
Acts 2. 37–end

R

or, if Matthias is celebrated on 24 February:

Acts 14. 5–18
Ps. 118. 1–3, 14–15
John 14. 21–26

Ps. 145
alt. Ps. 71
Deut. 16. 1–20
I Pet. 1. 1–12

W

16 Tu — Caroline Chisholm, Social Reformer, 1877

Acts 14. 19–end
Ps. 145. 10–end
John 14. 27–end

Ps. *19*; 147. 1–12
alt. Ps. 73
Deut. 17. 8–end
I Pet. 1. 13–end

W

17 W

Acts 15. 1–6
Ps. 122. 1–5
John 15. 1–8

Ps. *30*; 147. 13–end
alt. Ps. 77
Deut. 18. 9–end
I Pet. 2. 1–10

W

18 Th

Acts 15. 7–21
Ps. 96. 1–3, 7–10
John 15. 9–11

Ps. *57*; 148
alt. Ps. 78. 1–39†
Deut. ch. 19
I Pet. 2. 11–end

W

19 F — **Dunstan, Archbishop of Canterbury, Restorer of Monastic Life, 988**
Com. Bishop   *or*
esp. Matt. 24. 42–46
also Exod. 31. 1–5

Acts 15. 22–31
Ps. 57. 8–end
John 15. 12–17

Ps. *138*; 149
alt. Ps. 55
Deut. 21.22 – 22.8
I Pet. 3. 1–12

W

20 Sa — **Alcuin of York, Deacon, Abbot of Tours, 804**
Com. Religious   *or*
also Col. 3. 12–16
John 4. 19–24

Acts 16. 1–10
Ps. 100
John 15. 18–21

Ps. *146*; 150
alt. Ps. *76*; 79
Deut. 24. 5–end
I Pet. 3. 13–end

W

21 S — THE SIXTH SUNDAY OF EASTER
The reading from Acts must be used as either the first or second reading at the Principal Service.

Acts 17. 22–31
[or Gen. 8.20 – 9.17]
Ps. 66. 7–end
I Pet. 3. 13–end
John 14. 15–21

Ps. 73. 21–28
Job 14. 1–2, 7–15;
19. 23–27a
I Thess. 4. 13–end

W

22 M — Rogation Day**

Acts 16. 11–15
Ps. 149. 1–5
John 15.26 – 16.4

Ps. *65*; 67
alt. Ps. *80*; 82
Deut. ch. 26
I Pet. 4. 1–11

W

23 Tu — Rogation Day**

Acts 16. 22–34
Ps. 138
John 16. 5–11

Ps. 124; 125; *126*; 127
alt. Ps. 87; *89. 1–18*
Deut. 28. 1–14
I Pet. 4. 12–end

W

*Matthias may be celebrated on 24 February instead of 15 May.
**For Rogation Day provision, see p. 10.

Second Service Evening Prayer	Calendar and Holy Communion	Morning Prayer	Evening Prayer
	THE FOURTH SUNDAY AFTER EASTER		
Ps. 147. 1–12 Zech. 4. 1–10 Rev. 21. 1–14 *Gospel:* Luke 2. 25–32 [33–38] *or First EP of Matthias* Ps. 147 Isa. 22. 15–22 Phil. 3.13b – 4.1 **R ct**	Job 19. 21–27a Ps. 66. 14–end James 1. 17–21 John 16. 5–15 W	Ps. 30 Ezek. 37. 1–12 John 5. 19–29	Ps. 147. 1–12 Zech. 4. 1–10 Rev. 21. 1–14
EP: Ps. 80 1 Sam. 16. 1–13a Matt. 7. 15–27		Deut. 16. 1–20 1 Pet. 1. 1–12	Num. 9. 15–end; 10. 33–end Luke 4. 38–end
Ps. 105 *alt.* Ps. **72**; 75 Num. 9. 15–end; 10. 33–end Luke 4. 38–end	W		
Ps. 96; **97** *alt.* Ps. 74 Num. 11. 1–33 Luke 5. 1–11	W	Deut. 17. 8–end 1 Pet. 1. 13–end	Num. 11. 1–33 Luke 5. 1–11
Ps. 98; **99**; 100 *alt.* Ps. 119. 81–104 Num. ch. 12 Luke 5. 12–26	W	Deut. 18. 9–end 1 Pet. 2. 1–10	Num. ch. 12 Luke 5. 12–26
Ps. 104 *alt.* Ps. 78. 40–end† Num. 13. 1–3, 17–end Luke 5. 27–end	W	Deut. ch. 19 1 Pet. 2. 11–end	Num. 13. 1–3, 17–end Luke 5. 27–end
	Dunstan, Archbishop of Canterbury, Restorer of Monastic Life, 988		
Ps. 66 *alt.* Ps. 69 Num. 14. 1–25 Luke 6. 1–11	Com. Bishop W	Deut. 21.22 – 22.8 1 Pet. 3. 1–12	Num. 14. 1–25 Luke 6. 1–11
Ps. 118 *alt.* Ps. 81; **84** Num. 14. 26–end Luke 6. 12–26 ct	W	Deut. 24. 5–end 1 Pet. 3. 13–end	Num. 14. 26–end Luke 6. 12–26 ct
Ps. 87; 36. 5–10 Zech. 8. 1–13 Rev. 21.22 – 22.5 *Gospel:* John 21. 1–14	THE FIFTH SUNDAY AFTER EASTER Rogation Sunday Joel 2. 21–26 Ps. 66. 1–8 James 1. 22–end John 16. 23b–end W	Ps. 73. 21–28 Job 14. 1–2, 7–15; 19. 23–27a 1 Thess. 4. 13–end	Ps. 87; 36. 5–10 Zech. 8. 1–13 Rev. 21.22 – 22.5
Ps. *121*; 122; 123 *alt.* Ps. **85**; 86 Num. 16. 1–35 Luke 6. 27–38	Rogation Day Job 28. 1–11 Ps. 107. 1–9 James 5. 7–11 Luke 6. 36–42 W	Deut. ch. 26 1 Pet. 4. 1–11	Num. 16. 1–35 Luke 6. 27–38
Ps. *128*; 129; 130; 131 *alt.* Ps. 89. 19–end Num. 16. 36–end Luke 6. 39–end	Rogation Day Deut. 8. 1–10 Ps. 121 James 5. 16–end Luke 11. 5–13 W	Deut. 28. 1–14 1 Pet. 4. 12–end	Num. 16. 36–end Luke 6. 39–end

May 2017

			Sunday Principal Service / Weekday Eucharist	Third Service / Morning Prayer

24 W — **John and Charles Wesley, Evangelists, Hymn Writers, 1791 and 1788**
Rogation Day*
Com. Pastor
also Eph. 5. 15–20

or Acts 17.15, 22 – 18.1
Ps. 148. 1–2, 11–end
John 16. 12–15

Ps. *132*; 133
alt. Ps. 119. 105–128
Deut. 28. 58–end
1 Pet. ch. 5

W

25 Th — **ASCENSION DAY**
The reading from Acts must be used as either the first or second reading at the Eucharist.

Acts 1. 1–11
or Dan. 7. 9–14
Ps. 47 or Ps. 93
Eph. 1. 15–end
or Acts 1. 1–11
Luke 24. 44–end

MP: Ps. 110; 150
Isa. 52. 7–end
Heb. 7. [11–25] 26–end

₩

26 F — **Augustine, first Archbishop of Canterbury, 605**
John Calvin, Reformer, 1564; Philip Neri, Founder of the Oratorians, Spiritual Guide, 1595
Com. Bishop
also 1 Thess. 2. 2b–8
Matt. 13. 31–33

or Acts 18. 9–18
Ps. 47. 1–6
John 16. 20–23

Ps. 20; *81*
alt. Ps. *88*; (95)
Deut. 29. 2–15
1 John 1.1 – 2.6
[Exod. 35.30 – 36.1
Gal. 5. 13–end]**

W

27 Sa —

Acts 18. 22–end
Ps. 47. 1–2, 7–end
John 16. 23–28

Ps. 21; *47*
alt. Ps. 96; *97*; 100
Deut. ch. 30
1 John 2. 7–17
[Num. 11. 16–17, 24–29
1 Cor. ch. 2]

W

28 S — **THE SEVENTH SUNDAY OF EASTER (SUNDAY AFTER ASCENSION DAY)**
The reading from Acts must be used as either the first or second reading at the Principal Service.

Acts 1. 6–14
[or Ezek. 36. 24–28]
Ps. 68. 1–10, 32–end
(or 68. 1–10)
1 Pet. 4. 12–14; 5. 6–11
John 17. 1–11

Ps. 104. 26–35
Isa. 65. 17–end
Rev. 21. 1–8

W

29 M —

Acts 19. 1–8
Ps. 68. 1–6
John 16. 29–end

Ps. *93*; 96; 97
alt. Ps. *98*; 99; 101
Deut. 31. 1–13
1 John 2. 18–end
[Num. 27. 15–end
1 Cor. ch. 3]

W

30 Tu — **Josephine Butler, Social Reformer, 1906**
Joan of Arc, Visionary, 1431; Apolo Kivebulaya, Evangelist in Central Africa, 1933
Com. Saint
esp. Isa. 58. 6–11
also 1 John 3. 18–23
Matt. 9. 10–13

or Acts 20. 17–27
Ps. 68. 9–10, 18–19
John 17. 1–11

Ps. 98; *99*; 100
alt. Ps. *106*† (or 103)
Deut. 31. 14–29
1 John 3. 1–10
[1 Sam. 10. 1–10
1 Cor. 12. 1–13]

W

31 W — **THE VISIT OF THE BLESSED VIRGIN MARY TO ELIZABETH*****

Zeph. 3. 14–18
Ps. 113
Rom. 12. 9–16
Luke 1. 39–49 [50–56]

MP: Ps. 85; 150
1 Sam. 2. 1–10
Mark 3. 31–end

W

*For Rogation Day provision, see p. 10.
**The alternative readings in square brackets may be used at one of the offices, in preparation for the Day of Pentecost.
***The Visit of the Blessed Virgin Mary to Elizabeth may be celebrated on 2 July or transferred to 4 July or, if Thomas the Apostle is celebrated on 21 December, transferred to 3 July.

Second Service Evening Prayer		Calendar and Holy Communion	Morning Prayer	Evening Prayer
		Rogation Day		
First EP of Ascension Day Ps. 15; 24 2 Sam. 23. 1–5 Col. 2.20 – 3.4 ℟ ct	W	Deut. 34. 1–7 Ps. 108. 1–6 Eph. 4. 7–13 John 17. 1–11	Deut. 28. 58–end 1 Pet. ch. 5	First EP of Ascension Day Ps. 15; 24 2 Sam. 23. 1–5 Col. 2.20 – 3.4 ℟ ct
EP: Ps. 8 Song of the Three 29–37 or 2 Kings 2. 1–15 Rev. ch. 5 Gospel: Mark 16. 14–end	℟	**ASCENSION DAY** Dan. 7. 13–14 Ps. 68. 1–6 Acts 1. 1–11 Mark 16. 14–end or Luke 24. 44–end	Ps. 110; 150 Isa. 52. 7–end Heb. 7. [11–25] 26–end	Ps. 8 Song of the Three 29–37 or 2 Kings 2. 1–15 Rev. ch. 5
Ps. 145 alt. Ps. 102 Num. 20. 1–13 Luke 7. 11–17	W	**Augustine, first Archbishop of Canterbury, 605** Com. Bishop or Ascension CEG	Deut. 29. 2–15 1 John 1.1 – 2.6 [Exod. 35.30 – 36.1 Gal. 5. 13–end]**	Num. 20. 1–13 Luke 7. 11–17
Ps. 84; **85** alt. Ps. 104 Num. 21. 4–9 Luke 7. 18–35 ct	W	**The Venerable Bede, Monk at Jarrow, Scholar, Historian, 735** Com. Religious or Ascension CEG	Deut. ch. 30 1 John 2. 7–17 [Num. 11. 16–17, 24–29 1 Cor. ch. 2]	Num. 21. 4–9 Luke 7. 18–35 ct
Ps. 47 2 Sam. 23. 1–5 Eph. 1. 15–end Gospel: Mark 16. 14–end	W	THE SUNDAY AFTER ASCENSION DAY 2 Kings 2. 9–15 Ps. 68. 32–end 1 Pet. 4. 7–11 John 15.26 – 16.4a	Ps. 104. 26–35 Isa. 65. 17–end Rev. 21. 1–8	Ps. 47 2 Sam. 23. 1–5 Eph. 1. 15–end
Ps. 18 alt. Ps. **105**† (or 103) Num. 22. 1–35 Luke 7. 36–end	W		Deut. 31. 1–13 1 John 2. 18–end [Num. 27. 15–end 1 Cor. ch. 3]	Num. 22. 1–35 Luke 7. 36–end
Ps. 68 alt. Ps. 107† Num. 22.36 – 23.12 Luke 8. 1–15 or First EP of The Visit of Mary to Elizabeth Ps. 45 Song of Sol. 2. 8–14 Luke 1. 26–38 ct	W		Deut. 31. 14–29 1 John 3. 1–10 [1 Sam. 10. 1–10 1 Cor. 12. 1–13]	Num. 22.36 – 23.12 Luke 8. 1–15
EP: Ps. 122; 127; 128 Zech. 2. 10–end John 3. 25–30 *(Continued overleaf)*	W		Deut. 31.30 – 32.14 1 John 3. 11–end [1 Kings 19. 1–18 Matt. 3. 13–end]	Num. 23. 13–end Luke 8. 16–25

May 2017

			Sunday Principal Service Weekday Eucharist	Third Service Morning Prayer
		(Continued from pages 48 and 49)		
31	W	*or, if The Visitation is celebrated on 2, 3 or 4 July:*	Acts 20. 28–end Ps. 68. 27–28, 32–end John 17. 11–19	Ps. 2; **29** *alt.* Ps. 110; ***111***; 112 Deut. 31.30 – 32.14 1 John 3. 11–end [1 Kings 19. 1–18
	W			Matt. 3. 13–end]

June 2017

					Third Service Morning Prayer
1	Th	**Justin, Martyr at Rome, c. 165** Com. Martyr *esp.* John 15. 18–21 *also* 1 Macc. 2. 15–22 1 Cor. 1. 18–25	*or*	Acts 22. 30; 23. 6–11 Ps. 16. 1, 5–end John 17. 20–end	Ps. **24**; 72 *alt.* Ps. 113; ***115*** Deut. 32. 15–47 1 John 4. 1–6 [Ezek. 11. 14–20
	Wr				Matt. 9.35 – 10.20]
2	F			Acts 25. 13–21 Ps. 103. 1–2, 11–12, 19–20 John 21. 15–19	Ps. **28**; 30 *alt.* Ps. 139 Deut. ch. 33 1 John 4. 7–end [Ezek. 36. 22–28
	W				Matt. 12. 22–32]
3	Sa	*The Martyrs of Uganda, 1885–87 and 1977*		Acts 28. 16–20, 30–end Ps. 11. 4–end John 21. 20–end	Ps. 42; **43** *alt.* Ps. 120; ***121***; 122 Deut. 32. 48–end; ch. 34 1 John ch. 5 [Mic. 3. 1–8
	W				Eph. 6. 10–20]
4	S	**DAY OF PENTECOST (Whit Sunday)** *The reading from Acts must be used as either the first or second reading at the Principal Service.*		Acts 2. 1–21 *or* Num. 11. 24–30 Ps. 104. 26–36, 37b (*or* 104. 26–end) 1 Cor. 12. 3b–13 *or* Acts 2. 1–21 John 20. 19–23	MP: Ps. 87 Gen. 11. 1–9 Acts 10. 34–end
	R			*or* John 7. 37–39	
5 DEL 9	M	**Boniface (Wynfrith) of Crediton, Bishop, Apostle of Germany, Martyr, 754** Ordinary Time resumes today Com. Martyr *also* Acts 20. 24–28	*or*	Tob. 1. 1–2; 2. 1–8 *or* 1 Pet. 1. 3–9 Ps. 15 *or* Ps. 111	Ps. 123; 124; 125; ***126*** Job ch. 1 Rom. 1. 1–17
	Gr			Mark 12. 1–12	
6	Tu	*Ini Kopuria, Founder of the Melanesian Brotherhood, 1945*		Tob. 2. 9–end *or* 1 Pet. 1. 10–16 Ps. 112 *or* Ps. 98. 1–5	Ps. **132**; 133 Job ch. 2 Rom. 1. 18–end
	G			Mark 12. 13–17	
7	W			Tob. 3. 1–11, 16–end *or* 1 Pet. 1. 18–25 Ps. 25. 1–8 *or* Ps. 147. 13–end	Ps. 119. 153–end Job ch. 3 Rom. 2. 1–16
	G			Mark 12. 18–27	
8	Th	**Thomas Ken, Bishop of Bath and Wells, Nonjuror, Hymn Writer, 1711** Com. Bishop *esp.* 2 Cor. 4. 1–10 Matt. 24. 42–46	*or*	Tob. 6. 10–11; 7. 1–15; 8. 4–8 *or* 1 Pet. 2. 2–5, 9–12 Ps. 128 *or* Ps. 100	Ps. **143**; 146 Job ch. 4 Rom. 2. 17–end
	Gw			Mark 12. 28–34	

Second Service Evening Prayer		Calendar and Holy Communion	Morning Prayer	Evening Prayer
Ps. 36; **46** *alt.* Ps. 119. 129–152 Num. 23. 13–end Luke 8. 16–25	W			
		Nicomede, Priest and Martyr at Rome (date unknown)		
Ps. 139 *alt.* Ps. 114; **116**; 117 Num. ch. 24 Luke 8. 26–39	Wr	Com. Martyr	Deut. 32. 15–47 I John 4. 1–6 [Ezek. 11. 14–20 Matt. 9.35 – 10.20]	Num. ch. 24 Luke 8. 26–39
Ps. 147 *alt.* Ps. **130**; 131; 137 Num. 27. 12–end Luke 8. 40–end	W		Deut. ch. 33 I John 4. 7–end [Ezek. 36. 22–28 Matt. 12. 22–32]	Num. 27. 12–end Luke 8. 40–end
First EP of Pentecost Ps. 48 Deut. 16. 9–15 John 15.26 – 16.15 **R ct**	W		Deut. 32. 48–end; ch. 34 I John ch. 5 [Mic. 3. 1–8 Eph. 6. 10–20]	*First EP of Whit Sunday* Ps. 48 Deut. 16. 9–15 John 15.26 – 16.15 **R ct**
EP: Ps. 67; 133 Joel 2. 21–end Acts 2. 14–21 [22–38] *Gospel:* Luke 24. 44–end	R	**WHIT SUNDAY** Deut. 16. 9–12 Ps. 122 Acts 2. 1–11 John 14. 15–31a	Ps. 87 Gen. 11. 1–9 Acts 10. 34–end	Ps. 67; 133 Num. 11. 24–30 Acts 2. 14–21 [22–38]
		Monday in Whitsun Week		
Ps. **127**; 128; 129 Josh. ch. 1 Luke 9. 18–27	R	Acts 10. 34–end John 3. 16–21	Ezek. 11. 14–20 Acts 2. 12–36	Exod. 35.30 – 36.1 Acts 2. 37–end
		Tuesday in Whitsun Week		
Ps. (134); **135** Josh. ch. 2 Luke 9. 28–36	R	Acts 8. 14–17 John 10. 1–10	Ezek. 37. 1–14 I Cor. 12. 1–13	2 Sam. 23. 1–5 I Cor. 12.27 – 13.end
Ps. 136 Josh. ch. 3 Luke 9. 37–50	R	Ember Day Ember CEG *or* Acts 2. 14–21 John 6. 44–51	Job ch. 3 Rom. 2. 1–16	Josh. ch. 3 Luke 9. 37–50
Ps. **138**; 140; 141 Josh. 4.1 – 5.1 Luke 9. 51–end	R	Acts 2. 22–28 Luke 9. 1–6	Job ch. 4 Rom. 2. 17–end	Josh. 4.1 – 5.1 Luke 9. 51–end

June 2017

				Sunday Principal Service Weekday Eucharist	Third Service Morning Prayer

9 — F — **Columba, Abbot of Iona, Missionary, 597**
Ephrem of Syria, Deacon, Hymn Writer, Teacher, 373
Com. Missionary   *or*   Tob. 11. 5–15
also Titus 2. 11–end   *or* 1 Pet. 4. 7–13   Ps. *142*; 144
                                            Ps. 146   Job ch. 5
                                            or Ps. 96. 10–end   Rom. 3. 1–20
Gw   Mark 12. 35–37

10 — Sa
                                            Tob. 12. 1, 5–15, 20a   Ps. 147
                                            or Jude 17, 20–25   Job ch. 6
                                            Ps. 103. 1, 8–13   Rom. 3. 21–end
                                            or Ps. 63. 1–6
G   Mark 12. 38–end

11 — S — **TRINITY SUNDAY**
(Barnabas transferred to the 12th)
                                            Isa. 40. 12–17, 27–end   MP: Ps. 86. 8–13
                                            Ps. 8   Exod. 3. 1–6, 13–15
                                            2 Cor. 13. 11–end   John 17. 1–11
                                            Matt. 28. 16–20

〰

12 — M — **BARNABAS THE APOSTLE** (transferred from the 11th)
DEL 10   Job 29. 11–16   MP: Ps. 100; 101; 117
                                            or Acts 11. 19–end   Jer. 9. 23–24
                                            Ps. 112   Acts 4. 32–end
                                            Acts 11. 19–end
                                            or Gal. 2. 1–10
R   John 15. 12–17

13 — Tu
                                            2 Cor. 1. 18–22   Ps. *5*; 6; (8)
                                            Ps. 119. 129–136   Job ch. 8
G   Matt. 5. 13–16   Rom. 4. 13–end

14 — W — *Richard Baxter, Puritan Divine, 1691*
                                            2 Cor. 3. 4–11   Ps. 119. 1–32
                                            Ps. 78. 1–4   Job ch. 9
                                            Matt. 5. 17–19   Rom. 5. 1–11

G

15 — Th — **DAY OF THANKSGIVING FOR HOLY COMMUNION (CORPUS CHRISTI)**
Evelyn Underhill, Spiritual Writer, 1941
                                            Gen. 14. 18–20   MP: Ps. 147
                                            Ps. 116. 10–end   Deut. 8. 2–16
W   1 Cor. 11. 23–26   1 Cor. 10. 1–17
                                            John 6. 51–58
or the ferial readings for the day: 2 Cor. 3.15 – 4.1, 3–6   Ps. 14; *15*; 16
                                            Ps. 78. 36–40   Job. ch. 10
G   Matt. 5. 20–26   Rom. 5. 12–end

16 — F — **Richard, Bishop of Chichester, 1253**
Joseph Butler, Bishop of Durham, Philosopher, 1752
Com. Bishop   *or*   2 Cor. 4. 7–15   Ps. 17; *19*
also John 21. 15–19   Ps. 99   Job ch. 11
Gw   Matt. 5. 27–32   Rom. 6. 1–14

17 — Sa — *Samuel and Henrietta Barnett, Social Reformers, 1913 and 1936*
                                            2 Cor. 5. 14–end   Ps. 20; 21; *23*
                                            Ps. 103. 1–12   Job ch. 12
G   Matt. 5. 33–37   Rom. 6. 15–end

Second Service Evening Prayer	Calendar and Holy Communion	Morning Prayer	Evening Prayer
Ps. 145 Josh. 5. 2–end Luke 10. 1–16	Ember Day Ember CEG or Acts 8. 5–8 Luke 5. 17–26 **R**	Job ch. 5 Rom. 3. 1–20	Josh. 5. 2–end Luke 10. 1–16
First EP of Trinity Sunday Ps. 97; 98 Exod. 34. 1–10 Mark 1. 1–13 𝕎 ct	Ember Day Ember CEG or Acts 13. 44–end Matt. 20. 29–end **R**	Job ch. 6 Rom. 3. 21–end	*First EP of Trinity Sunday* Ps. 97; 98 Exod. 34. 1–10 Mark 1. 1–13 𝕎 ct
EP: Ps. 93; 150 Isa. 6. 1–8 John 16. 5–15 *or First EP of Barnabas* Ps. 1; 15 Isa. 42. 5–12 Acts 14. 8–end **R ct**	**TRINITY SUNDAY** (Barnabas transferred to the 12th) Isa. 6. 1–8 Ps. 8 Rev. 4. 1–11 John 3. 1–15 𝕎	Ps. 86. 8–13 Exod. 3. 1–6, 13–15 John 17. 1–11	Ps. 93; 150 Isa. 40. 12–17, 27–end John 16. 5–15 *or First EP of Barnabas* Ps. 1; 15 Isa. 42. 5–12 Acts 14. 8–end **R ct**
EP: Ps. 147 Eccles. 12. 9–end or Tobit 4. 5–11 Acts 9. 26–31	**BARNABAS THE APOSTLE** (transferred from the 11th) Job 29. 11–16 Ps. 112 Acts 11. 22–end John 15. 12–16 **R**	(Ps. 100; 101; 117) Jer. 9. 23–24 Acts 4. 32–end	(Ps. 147) Eccles. 12. 9–end or Tobit 4. 5–11 Acts 9. 26–31
Ps. *9*; 10† Josh. 7. 16–end Luke 10. 38–end	**G**	Job ch. 8 Rom. 4. 13–end	Josh. 7. 16–end Luke 10. 38–end
Ps. *11*; 12; 13 Josh. 8. 1–29 Luke 11. 1–13 *or First EP of Corpus Christi* Ps. 110; 111 Exod. 16. 2–15 John 6. 22–35 **W ct**	**G**	Job ch. 9 Rom. 5. 1–11	Josh. 8. 1–29 Luke 11. 1–13
	To celebrate Corpus Christi, see *Common Worship* provision.		
EP: Ps. 23; 42; 43 Prov. 9. 1–5 Luke 9. 11–17		Job. ch. 10 Rom. 5. 12–end	Josh. 8. 30–end Luke 11. 14–28
Ps. 18† Josh. 8. 30–end Luke 11. 14–28	**G**		
Ps. 22 Josh. 9. 3–26 Luke 11. 29–36	**G**	Job ch. 11 Rom. 6. 1–14	Josh. 9. 3–26 Luke 11. 29–36
Ps. *24*; 25 Josh. 10. 1–15 Luke 11. 37–end ct	**Alban, first Martyr of Britain, c. 250** Com. Martyr **Gr**	Job ch. 12 Rom. 6. 15–end	Josh. 10. 1–15 Luke 11. 37–end ct

June 2017

			Sunday Principal Service / Weekday Eucharist	Third Service / Morning Prayer

18 S — THE FIRST SUNDAY AFTER TRINITY (Proper 6)
Track 1
Gen. 18. 1–15 [21. 1–7]
Ps. 116. 1, 10–17 (or 116. 9–17)
Rom. 5. 1–8
G — Matt. 9.35 – 10.8 [9–23]

Track 2
Exod. 19. 2–8a
Ps. 100
Rom. 5. 1–8
Matt. 9.35 – 10.8 [9–23]

Ps. 45
Deut. 10.12 – 11.1
Acts 23. 12–end

19 M — *Sundar Singh of India, Sadhu (holy man), Evangelist, Teacher, 1929*
DEL 11
2 Cor. 6. 1–10
Ps. 98
G — Matt. 5. 38–42

Ps. 27; **30**
Job ch. 13
Rom. 7. 1–6

20 Tu
2 Cor. 8. 1–9
Ps. 146
G — Matt. 5. 43–end

Ps. 32; **36**
Job ch. 14
Rom. 7. 7–end

21 W
2 Cor. 9. 6–11
Ps. 112
G — Matt. 6. 1–6, 16–18

Ps. 34
Job ch. 15
Rom. 8. 1–11

22 Th — **Alban, first Martyr of Britain, c. 250**
Com. Martyr   *or*   2 Cor. 11. 1–11
esp. 2 Tim. 2. 3–13   Ps. 111
Gr — John 12. 24–26   Matt. 6. 7–15

Ps. 37†
Job 16.1 – 17.2
Rom. 8. 12–17

23 F — **Etheldreda, Abbess of Ely, c. 678**
Com. Religious   *or*   2 Cor. 11. 18, 21b–30
also Matt. 25. 1–13   Ps. 34. 1–6
Matt. 6. 19–23

Ps. 31
Job 17. 3–end
Rom. 8. 18–30

Gw

24 Sa — THE BIRTH OF JOHN THE BAPTIST
Isa. 40. 1–11
Ps. 85. 7–end
Acts 13. 14b–26
or Gal. 3. 23–end
W — Luke 1. 57–66, 80

MP: Ps. 50; 149
Ecclus. 48. 1–10
or Mal. 3. 1–6
Luke 3. 1–17

25 S — THE SECOND SUNDAY AFTER TRINITY (Proper 7)
Track 1
Gen. 21. 8–21
Ps. 86. 1–10, 16–end (or 86. 1–10)
Rom. 6. 1b–11
Matt. 10. 24–39
G

Track 2
Jer. 20. 7–13
Ps. 69. 8–11 [12–17] 18–40
(or 69. 14–20)
Rom. 6. 1b–11
Matt. 10. 24–39

Ps. 49
Deut. 11. 1–15
Acts 27. 1–12

26 M
DEL 12
Gen. 12. 1–9
Ps. 33. 12–end
G — Matt. 7. 1–5

Ps. 44
Job ch. 19
Rom. 9. 1–18

27 Tu — *Cyril, Bishop of Alexandria, Teacher, 444*
Gen. 13. 2, 5–end
Ps. 15
G — Matt. 7. 6, 12–14

Ps. **48**; 52
Job ch. 21
Rom. 9. 19–end

28 W — **Irenaeus, Bishop of Lyons, Teacher, c. 200**
Ember Day*
Com. Teacher   *or*   Gen. 15. 1–12, 17–18
also 2 Pet. 1. 16–end   Ps. 105. 1–9
Matt. 7. 15–20

Ps. 119. 57–80
Job ch. 22
Rom. 10. 1–10

Gw *or* Rw

*For Ember Day provision, see p. 11.

Second Service Evening Prayer	Calendar and Holy Communion		Morning Prayer	Evening Prayer
			THE FIRST SUNDAY AFTER TRINITY	
Ps. [42]; 43 1 Sam. 21. 1–15 Luke 11. 14–28		G	2 Sam. 9. 6–end Ps. 41. 1–4 1 John 4. 7–end Luke 16. 19–31	Ps. 45 Deut. 10.12 – 11.1 Acts 23. 12–end	Ps. [42]; 43 1 Sam. 21. 1–15 Luke 11. 14–28
Ps. 26; *28*; 29 Josh. ch. 14 Luke 12. 1–12		G		Job ch. 13 Rom. 7. 1–6	Josh. ch. 14 Luke 12. 1–12
Ps. 33 Josh. 21.43 – 22.8 Luke 12. 13–21	**Translation of Edward, King of the West Saxons, 979** Com. Martyr	Gr	Job ch. 14 Rom. 7. 7–end	Josh. 21.43 – 22.8 Luke 12. 13–21
Ps. 119. 33–56 Josh. 22. 9–end Luke 12. 22–31		G		Job ch. 15 Rom. 8. 1–11	Josh. 22. 9–end Luke 12. 22–31
Ps. 39; *40* Josh. ch. 23 Luke 12. 32–40		G		Job 16.1 – 17.2 Rom. 8. 12–17	Josh. ch. 23 Luke 12. 32–40
Ps. 35 Josh. 24. 1–28 Luke 12. 41–48 or First EP of The Birth of John the Baptist Ps. 71 Judg. 13. 2–7, 24–end Luke 1. 5–25 **W ct**		G		Job 17. 3–end Rom. 8. 18–30	Josh. 24. 1–28 Luke 12. 41–48 or First EP of The Nativity of John the Baptist (Ps. 71) Judg. 13. 2–7, 24–end Luke 1. 5–25 **W ct**
EP: Ps. 80; 82 Mal. ch. 4 Matt. 11. 2–19	**THE NATIVITY OF JOHN THE BAPTIST** Isa. 40. 1–11 Ps. 80. 1–7 Acts 13. 22–26 Luke 1. 57–80	W	(Ps. 50; 149) Ecclus. 48. 1–10 or Mal. 3. 1–6 Luke 3. 1–17	(Ps. 82) Mal. ch. 4 Matt. 11. 2–19
			THE SECOND SUNDAY AFTER TRINITY	
Ps. 46; [48] 1 Sam. 24. 1–17 Luke 14. 12–24	Gen. 12. 1–4 Ps. 120 1 John 3. 13–end Luke 14. 16–24	G	Ps. 49 Deut. 11. 1–15 Acts 27. 1–12	Ps. 46; [48] 1 Sam. 24. 1–17 Luke 14. 1–14
Ps. *47*; 49 Judg. ch. 2 Luke 13. 1–9		G	Job ch. 19 Rom. 9. 1–18	Judg. ch. 2 Luke 13. 1–9
Ps. 50 Judg. 4. 1–23 Luke 13. 10–21		G	Job ch. 21 Rom. 9. 19–end	Judg. 4. 1–23 Luke 13. 10–21
Ps. *59*; 60; (67) Judg. ch. 5 Luke 13. 22–end or First EP of Peter and Paul Ps. 66; 67 Ezek. 3. 4–11 Gal. 1.13 – 2.8 or, for Peter alone: Acts 9. 32–end **R ct**		G	Job ch. 22 Rom. 10. 1–10	Judg. ch. 5 Luke 13. 22–end or First EP of Peter (Ps. 66; 67) Ezek. 3. 4–11 Acts 9. 32–end **R ct**

June 2017

			Sunday Principal Service Weekday Eucharist	Third Service Morning Prayer
29	Th	PETER AND PAUL, APOSTLES	Zech. 4. 1–6a, 10b–end or Acts 12. 1–11 Ps. 125 Acts 12. 1–11 or 2 Tim. 4. 6–8, 17–18 Matt. 16. 13–19	MP: Ps. 71; 113 Isa. 49. 1–6 Acts 11. 1–18
	R	or, if Peter is commemorated alone:	Ezek. 3. 22–end or Acts 12. 1–11 Ps. 125 Acts 12. 1–11 or 1 Pet. 2. 19–end Matt. 16. 13–19	MP: Ps. 71; 113 Isa. 49. 1–6 Acts 11. 1–18
	R			
30	F	Ember Day*	Gen. 17. 1, 9–10, 15–22 Ps. 128 Matt. 8. 1–4	Ps. *51*; 54 Job ch. 24 Rom. 11. 1–12
	G or R			

July 2017

			Sunday Principal Service Weekday Eucharist	Third Service Morning Prayer
1	Sa	Ember Day* *Henry, John and Henry Venn the Younger, Priests, Evangelical Divines, 1797, 1813 and 1873*	Gen. 18. 1–15 Canticle: Luke 1. 46b–55 Matt. 8. 5–17	Ps. 68 Job chs 25 & 26 Rom. 11. 13–24
	G or R			
2	S	THE THIRD SUNDAY AFTER TRINITY (**Proper 8**)** Track 1 Gen. 22. 1–14 Ps. 13 Rom. 6. 12–end Matt. 10. 40–end	Track 2 Jer. 28. 5–9 Ps. 89. 1–4, 15–18 (or 89. 8–18) Rom. 6. 12–end Matt. 10. 40–end	Ps. 52; 53 Deut. 15. 1–11 Acts 27. [13–32] 33–end
	G			
3 DEL 13	M	THOMAS THE APOSTLE***	Hab. 2. 1–4 Ps. 31. 1–6 Eph. 2. 19–end John 20. 24–29	MP: Ps. 92; 146 2 Sam. 15. 17–21 or Ecclus. ch. 2 John 11. 1–16
	R	or, if Thomas is not celebrated:	Gen. 18. 16–end Ps. 103. 6–17 Matt. 8. 18–22	Ps. 71 Job ch. 27 Rom. 11. 25–end
	G			
4	Tu		Gen. 19. 15–29 Ps. 26 Matt. 8. 23–27	Ps. 73 Job ch. 28 Rom. 12. 1–8
	G			
5	W		Gen. 21. 5, 8–20 Ps. 34. 1–12 Matt. 8. 28–end	Ps. 77 Job ch. 29 Rom. 12. 9–end
	G			
6	Th	*Thomas More, Scholar, and John Fisher, Bishop of Rochester, Reformation Martyrs, 1535*	Gen. 22. 1–19 Ps. 116. 1–7 Matt. 9. 1–8	Ps. 78. 1–39† Job ch. 30 Rom. 13. 1–7
	G			
7	F****		Gen. 23. 1–4, 19; 24. 1–8, 62–end Ps. 106. 1–5 Matt. 9. 9–13	Ps. 55 Job ch. 31 Rom. 13. 8–end
	G			

*For Ember Day provision, see p. 11.
**The Visit of the Blessed Virgin Mary to Elizabeth may be celebrated on 2 July or transferred to 3 July (if Thomas the Apostle is celebrated on 21 December) or 4 July instead of 31 May.
***Thomas the Apostle may be celebrated on 21 December instead of 3 July.
****Thomas Becket may be celebrated on 7 July instead of 29 December.

Second Service Evening Prayer		Calendar and Holy Communion	Morning Prayer	Evening Prayer
EP: Ps. 124; 138 Ezek. 34. 11–16 John 21. 15–22		**PETER THE APOSTLE** Ezek. 3. 4–11 Ps. 125 Acts 12. 1–11 Matt. 16. 13–19	(Ps. 71; 113) Isa. 49. 1–6 Acts 11. 1–18	(Ps. 124; 138) Ezek. 34. 11–16 John 21. 15–22
EP: Ps. 124; 138 Ezek. 34. 11–16 John 21. 15–22	R			
Ps. 38 Judg. 6. 25–end Luke 14. 12–24	G		Job ch. 24 Rom. 11. 1–12	Judg. 6. 25–end Luke 14. 12–24
Ps. 65; **66** Judg. ch. 7 Luke 14. 25–end ct	G		Job chs 25 & 26 Rom. 11. 13–24	Judg. ch. 7 Luke 14. 25–end ct
Ps. 50 (or 50. 1–15) 1 Sam. 28. 3–19 Luke 17. 20–end *or First EP of Thomas* Ps. 27 Isa. ch. 35 Heb. 10.35 – 11.1 **R ct**	G	**THE THIRD SUNDAY AFTER TRINITY** 2 Chron. 33. 9–13 Ps. 55. 17–23 1 Pet. 5. 5b–11 Luke 15. 1–10	Ps. 52; 53 Deut. 15. 1–11 Acts 27. [13–32] 33–end	Ps. 50 (or 50. 1–15) 1 Sam. 28. 3–19 Luke 17. 20–end
EP: Ps. 139 Job 42. 1–6 1 Pet. 1. 3–12	G		Job ch. 27 Rom. 11. 25–end	Judg. 8. 22–end Luke 15. 1–10
Ps. **72**; 75 Judg. 8. 22–end Luke 15. 1–10				
Ps. 74 Judg. 9. 1–21 Luke 15. 11–end	Gw	**Translation of Martin, Bishop of Tours, c. 397** Com. Bishop	Job ch. 28 Rom. 12. 1–8	Judg. 9. 1–21 Luke 15. 11–end
Ps. 119. 81–104 Judg. 9. 22–end Luke 16. 1–18	G		Job ch. 29 Rom. 12. 9–end	Judg. 9. 22–end Luke 16. 1–18
Ps. 78. 40–end† Judg. 11. 1–11 Luke 16. 19–end	G		Job ch. 30 Rom. 13. 1–7	Judg. 11. 1–11 Luke 16. 19–end
Ps. 69 Judg. 11. 29–end Luke 17. 1–10	G		Job ch. 31 Rom. 13. 8–end	Judg. 11. 29–end Luke 17. 1–10

July 2017

		Sunday Principal Service Weekday Eucharist	Third Service Morning Prayer
8	Sa	Gen. 27. 1–5a, 15–29 Ps. 135. 1–6 Matt. 9. 14–17	Ps. **76**; 79 Job ch. 32 Rom. 14. 1–12
	G		
9	S	**THE FOURTH SUNDAY AFTER TRINITY (Proper 9)**	
		Track 1 Gen. 24. 34–38, 42–49, 58–end Ps. 45. 10–end *or Canticle*: Song of Sol. 2. 8–13 Rom. 7. 15–25a	*Track 2* Zech. 9. 9–12 Ps. 145. 8–15 Rom. 7. 15–25a Matt. 11. 16–19, 25–30	Ps. 55. 1–15, 18–22 Deut. 24. 10–end Acts 28. 1–16
	G	Matt. 11. 16–19, 25–end	
10 DEL 14	M	Gen. 28. 10–end Ps. 91. 1–10 Matt. 9. 18–26	Ps. **80**; 82 Job ch. 33 Rom. 14. 13–end
	G		
11	Tu	**Benedict of Nursia, Abbot of Monte Cassino, Father of Western Monasticism, c. 550**	
		Com. Religious *or* *also* 1 Cor. 3. 10–11	Gen. 32. 22–end Ps. 17. 1–8	Ps. 87; **89. 1–18** Job ch. 38
	Gw	Luke 18. 18–22	Matt. 9. 32–end	Rom. 15. 1–13
12	W	Gen. 41. 55–end; 42. 5–7, 17–end Ps. 33. 1–4, 18–end Matt. 10. 1–7	Ps. 119. 105–128 Job ch. 39 Rom. 15. 14–21
	G		
13	Th	Gen. 44. 18–21, 23–29; 45. 1–5 Ps. 105. 11–17 Matt. 10. 7–15	Ps. 90; **92** Job ch. 40 Rom. 15. 22–end
	G		
14	F	**John Keble, Priest, Tractarian, Poet, 1866**	
		Com. Pastor *or* *also* Lam. 3. 19–26	Gen. 46. 1–7, 28–30 Ps. 37. 3–6, 27–28	Ps. **88**; (95) Job ch. 41
	Gw	Matt. 5. 1–8	Matt. 10. 16–23	Rom. 16. 1–16
15	Sa	**Swithun, Bishop of Winchester, c. 862**	
		Bonaventure, Friar, Bishop, Teacher, 1274 Com. Bishop *or* *also* James 5. 7–11, 13–18	Gen. 49. 29–end; 50. 15–25 Ps. 105. 1–7 Matt. 10. 24–33	Ps. 96; **97**; 100 Job ch. 42 Rom. 16. 17–end
	Gw		
16	S	**THE FIFTH SUNDAY AFTER TRINITY (Proper 10)**	
		Track 1 Gen. 25. 19–end Ps. 119. 105–112 Rom. 8. 1–11	*Track 2* Isa. 55. 10–13 Ps. 65 (or 65. 8–end) Rom. 8. 1–11 Matt. 13. 1–9, 18–23	Ps. 64; 65 Deut. 28. 1–14 Acts 28. 17–end
	G	Matt. 13. 1–9, 18–23	
17 DEL 15	M	Exod. 1. 8–14, 22 Ps. 124 Matt. 10.34 – 11.1	Ps. **98**; 99; 101 Ezek. 1. 1–14 2 Cor. 1. 1–14
	G		
18	Tu	*Elizabeth Ferard, first Deaconess of the Church of England, Founder of the Community of St Andrew, 1883*	
		Exod. 2. 1–15 Ps. 69. 1–2, 31–end Matt. 11. 20–24	Ps. **106**†; (or 103) Ezek. 1.15 – 2.2 2 Cor. 1.15 – 2.4
	G		
19	W	**Gregory, Bishop of Nyssa, and his sister Macrina, Deaconess, Teachers, c. 394 and c. 379**	
		Com. Teacher *or* *esp.* 1 Cor. 2. 9–13	Exod. 3. 1–6, 9–12 Ps. 103. 1–7	Ps. 110; **111**; 112 Ezek. 2.3 – 3.11
	Gw	*also* Wisd. 9. 13–17	Matt. 11. 25–27	2 Cor. 2. 5–end
20	Th	*Margaret of Antioch, Martyr, 4th century; Bartolomé de las Casas, Apostle to the Indies, 1566*	
		Exod. 3. 13–20 Ps. 105. 1, 5, 8–9, 24–27 Matt. 11. 28–end	Ps. 113; **115** Ezek. 3. 12–end 2 Cor. ch. 3
	G		
21	F	Exod. 11.10 – 12.14 Ps. 116. 10–end Matt. 12. 1–8	Ps. 139 Ezek. ch. 8 2 Cor. ch. 4
	G		

Second Service Evening Prayer	Calendar and Holy Communion	Morning Prayer	Evening Prayer
Ps. 81; *84* Judg. 12. 1–7 Luke 17. 11–19 ct	G	Job ch. 32 Rom. 14. 1–12	Judg. 12. 1–7 Luke 17. 11–19 ct
	THE FOURTH SUNDAY AFTER TRINITY		
Ps. 56; [57] 2 Sam. 2. 1–11; 3. 1 Luke 18.31 – 19.10	Gen. 3. 17–19 Ps. 79. 8–10 Rom. 8. 18–23 Luke 6. 36–42 G	Ps. 55. 1–15, 18–22 Deut. 24. 10–end Acts 28. 1–16	Ps. 56; [57] 2 Sam. 2. 1–11; 3. 1 Luke 18.31 – 19.10
Ps. *85*; 86 Judg. 13. 1–24 Luke 17. 20–end	G	Job ch. 33 Rom. 14. 13–end	Judg. 13. 1–24 Luke 17. 20–end
Ps. 89. 19–end Judg. ch. 14 Luke 18. 1–14	G	Job ch. 38 Rom. 15. 1–13	Judg. ch. 14 Luke 18. 1–14
Ps. *91*; 93 Judg. 15.1 – 16.3 Luke 18. 15–30	G	Job ch. 39 Rom. 15. 14–21	Judg. 15.1 – 16.3 Luke 18. 15–30
Ps. 94 Judg. 16. 4–end Luke 18. 31–end	G	Job ch. 40 Rom. 15. 22–end	Judg. 16. 4–end Luke 18. 31–end
Ps. 102 Judg. ch. 17 Luke 19. 1–10	G	Job ch. 41 Rom. 16. 1–16	Judg. ch. 17 Luke 19. 1–10
Ps. 104 Judg. 18. 1–20, 27–end Luke 19. 11–27 ct	**Swithun, Bishop of Winchester, c. 862** Com. Bishop Gw	Job ch. 42 Rom. 16. 17–end	Judg. 18. 1–20, 27–end Luke 19. 11–27 ct
	THE FIFTH SUNDAY AFTER TRINITY		
Ps. 60; [63] 2 Sam. 7. 18–end Luke 19.41 – 20.8	I Kings 19. 19–21 Ps. 84. 8–end I Pet. 3. 8–15a Luke 5. 1–11 G	Ps. 64; 65 Deut. 28. 1–14 Acts 28. 17–end	Ps. 60; [63] 2 Sam. 7. 18–end Luke 20. 1–8
Ps. *105*† (or 103) I Sam. 1. 1–20 Luke 19. 28–40	G	Ezek. 1. 1–14 2 Cor. 1. 1–14	I Sam. 1. 1–20 Luke 19. 28–40
Ps. 107† I Sam. 1.21 – 2.11 Luke 19. 41–end	G	Ezek. 1.15 – 2.2 2 Cor. 1.15 – 2.4	I Sam. 1.21 – 2.11 Luke 19. 41–end
Ps. 119. 129–152 I Sam. 2. 12–26 Luke 20. 1–8	G	Ezek. 2.3 – 3.11 2 Cor. 2. 5–end	I Sam. 2. 12–26 Luke 20. 1–8
Ps. 114; *116*; 117 I Sam. 2. 27–end Luke 20. 9–19	**Margaret of Antioch, Martyr, 4th century** Com. Virgin Martyr Gr	Ezek. 3. 12–end 2 Cor. ch. 3	I Sam. 2. 27–end Luke 20. 9–19
Ps. *130*; 131; 137 I Sam. 3.1 – 4.1a Luke 20. 20–26 *or First EP of Mary Magdalene* Ps. 139 Isa. 25. 1–9 2 Cor. 1. 3–7 **W** ct	G	Ezek. ch. 8 2 Cor. ch. 4	I Sam. 3.1 – 4.1a Luke 20. 20–26 *or First EP of Mary Magdalene* (Ps. 139) Isa. 25. 1–9 2 Cor. 1. 3–7 **W** ct

July 2017

			Sunday Principal Service / Weekday Eucharist	Third Service / Morning Prayer

22 Sa — MARY MAGDALENE
W

Sunday Principal Service / Weekday Eucharist	Third Service / Morning Prayer
Song of Sol. 3. 1–4 Ps. 42. 1–10 2 Cor. 5. 14–17 John 20. 1–2, 11–18	*MP*: Ps. 30; 32; 150 I Sam. 16. 14–end Luke 8. 1–3

23 S — THE SIXTH SUNDAY AFTER TRINITY (Proper 11)
G

Track 1 Gen. 28. 10–19a Ps. 139. 1–11, 23–24 (*or* 139. 1–11) Rom. 8. 12–25 Matt. 13. 24–30, 36–43	*Track 2* Wisd. 12. 13, 16–19 *or* Isa. 44. 6–8 Ps. 86. 11–end Rom. 8. 12–25 Matt. 13. 24–30, 36–43	Ps. 71 Deut. 30. 1–10 I Pet. 3. 8–18

24 M
DEL 16
G

Exod. 14. 5–18 Ps. 136. 1–4, 10–15 *or Canticle*: Exod. 15. 1–6 Matt. 12. 38–42	Ps. 123; 124; 125; *126* Ezek. 10. 1–19 2 Cor. 6.1 – 7.1

25 Tu — JAMES THE APOSTLE
R

Jer. 45. 1–5 *or* Acts 11.27 – 12.2 Ps. 126 Acts 11.27 – 12.2 *or* 2 Cor. 4. 7–15 Matt. 20. 20–28	*MP*: Ps. 7; 29; 117 2 Kings 1. 9–15 Luke 9. 46–56

26 W — **Anne and Joachim, Parents of the Blessed Virgin Mary**
Gw

Zeph. 3. 14–18a Ps. 127 Rom. 8. 28–30 Matt. 13. 16–17	*or*	Exod. 16. 1–5, 9–15 Ps. 78. 17–31 Matt. 13. 1–9	Ps. 119. 153–end Ezek. 12. 1–16 2 Cor. 8. 1–15

27 Th — *Brooke Foss Westcott, Bishop of Durham, Teacher, 1901*
G

Exod. 19. 1–2, 9–11, 16–20 *Canticle*: Bless the Lord Matt. 13. 10–17	Ps. *143*; 146 Ezek. 12. 17–end 2 Cor. 8.16 – 9.5

28 F
G

Exod. 20. 1–17 Ps. 19.7–11 Matt. 13. 18–23	Ps. 142; *144* Ezek. 13. 1–16 2 Cor. 9. 6–end

29 Sa — **Mary, Martha and Lazarus, Companions of Our Lord**
Gw

Isa. 25. 6–9 Ps. 49. 5–10, 16 Heb. 2. 10–15 John 12. 1–8	*or*	Exod. 24. 3–8 Ps. 50. 1–6, 14–15 Matt. 13. 24–30	Ps. 147 Ezek. 14. 1–11 2 Cor. ch. 10

30 S — THE SEVENTH SUNDAY AFTER TRINITY (Proper 12)
G

Track 1 Gen. 29. 15–28 Ps. 105. 1–11, 45b (*or* 105. 1–11) *or* Ps. 128 Rom. 8. 26–end Matt. 13. 31–33, 44–52	*Track 2* I Kings 3. 5–12 Ps. 119. 129–136 Rom. 8. 26–39 Matt. 13. 31–33, 44–52	Ps. 77 Song of Sol. ch. 2 *or* I Macc. 2. [1–14] 15–22 I Pet. 4. 7–14

31 M — *Ignatius of Loyola, Founder of the Society of Jesus, 1556*
DEL 17
G

Exod. 32. 15–24, 30–34 Ps. 106. 19–23 Matt. 13. 31–35	Ps. *1*; 2; 3 Ezek. 14. 12–end 2 Cor. 11. 1–15

August 2017

1 Tu
G

Exod. 33. 7–11; 34. 5–9, 28 Ps. 103. 8–12 Matt. 13. 36–43	Ps. *5*; 6; (8) Ezek. 18. 1–20 2 Cor. 11. 16–end

2 W
G

Exod. 34. 29–end Ps. 99 Matt. 13. 44–46	Ps. 119. 1–32 Ezek. 18. 21–32 2 Cor. ch. 12

Second Service Evening Prayer		Calendar and Holy Communion	Morning Prayer	Evening Prayer
EP: Ps. 63 Zeph. 3. 14–end Mark 15.40 – 16.7	W	**MARY MAGDALENE** Zeph. 3. 14–end Ps. 30. 1–5 2 Cor. 5. 14–17 John 20. 11–18	(Ps. 30; 32; 150) 1 Sam. 16. 14–end Luke 8. 1–3	(Ps. 63) Song of Sol. 3. 1–4 Mark 15.40 – 16.7
Ps. 67; [70] 1 Kings 2. 10–12; 3. 16–end Acts 4. 1–22 *Gospel:* Mark 6. 30–34, 53–end	G	**THE SIXTH SUNDAY AFTER TRINITY** Gen. 4. 2b–15 Ps. 90. 12–end Rom. 6. 3–11 Matt. 5. 20–26	Ps. 71 Deut. 30. 1–10 1 Pet. 3. 13–22	Ps. 67; [70] 1 Kings 2. 10–12; 3. 16–end Acts 4. 1–22
Ps. *127*; 128; 129 1 Sam. ch. 5 Luke 20.41 – 21.4 *or First EP of James* Ps. 144 Deut. 30. 11–end Mark 5. 21–end **R ct**	G		Ezek. 10. 1–19 2 Cor. 6.1 – 7.1	1 Sam. ch. 5 Luke 20.41 – 21.4 *or First EP of James* (Ps. 144) Deut. 30. 11–end Mark 5. 21–end **R ct**
EP: Ps. 94 Jer. 26. 1–15 Mark 1. 14–20	R	**JAMES THE APOSTLE** 2 Kings 1. 9–15 Ps. 15 Acts 11.27 – 12.3a Matt. 20. 20–28	(Ps. 7; 29; 117) Jer. 45. 1–5 Luke 9. 46–56	(Ps. 94) Jer. 26. 1–15 Mark 1. 14–20
Ps. 136 1 Sam. ch. 7 Luke 21. 20–28	Gw	**Anne, Mother of the Blessed Virgin Mary** Com. Saint	Ezek. 12. 1–16 2 Cor. 8. 1–15	1 Sam. ch. 7 Luke 21. 20–28
Ps. *138*; 140; 141 1 Sam. ch. 8 Luke 21. 29–end	G		Ezek. 12. 17–end 2 Cor. 8.16 – 9.5	1 Sam. ch. 8 Luke 21. 29–end
Ps. 145 1 Sam. 9. 1–14 Luke 22. 1–13	G		Ezek. 13. 1–16 2 Cor. 9. 6–end	1 Sam. 9. 1–14 Luke 22. 1–13
Ps. *148*; 149; 150 1 Sam. 9.15 – 10.1 Luke 22. 14–23 **ct**	G		Ezek. 14. 1–11 2 Cor. ch. 10	1 Sam. 9.15 – 10.1 Luke 22. 14–23 **ct**
Ps. 75; [76] 1 Kings 6. 11–14, 23–end Acts 12. 1–17 *Gospel:* John 6. 1–21	G	**THE SEVENTH SUNDAY AFTER TRINITY** 1 Kings 17. 8–16 Ps. 34. 11–end Rom. 6. 19–end Mark 8. 1–10a	Ps. 77 Song of Sol. ch. 2 *or* 1 Macc. 2. [1–14] 15–22 1 Pet. 4. 7–14	Ps. 75; [76] 1 Kings 6. 11–14, 23–end Acts 12. 1–17
Ps. 4; 7 1 Sam. 10. 1–16 Luke 22. 24–30	G		Ezek. 14. 12–end 2 Cor. 11. 1–15	1 Sam. 10. 1–16 Luke 22. 24–30
Ps. *9*; 10† 1 Sam. 10. 17–end Luke 22. 31–38	G	Lammas Day	Ezek. 18. 1–20 2 Cor. 11. 16–end	1 Sam. 10. 17–end Luke 22. 31–38
Ps. *11*; 12; 13 1 Sam. ch. 11 Luke 22. 39–46	G		Ezek. 18. 21–32 2 Cor. ch. 12	1 Sam. ch. 11 Luke 22. 39–46

August 2017

			Sunday Principal Service Weekday Eucharist	Third Service Morning Prayer
3	Th		Exod. 40. 16–21, 34–end Ps. 84. 1–6	Ps. 14; *15*; 16 Ezek. 20. 1–20
	G		Matt. 13. 47–53	2 Cor. ch. 13
4	F	*John-Baptiste Vianney, Curé d'Ars, Spiritual Guide, 1859*	Lev. 23. 1, 4–11, 15–16, 27, 34–37 Ps. 81. 1–8	Ps. 17; *19* Ezek. 20. 21–38 James 1. 1–11
	G		Matt. 13. 54–end	
5	Sa	**Oswald, King of Northumbria, Martyr, 642**		
		Com. Martyr *or* *esp.* 1 Pet. 4. 12–end John 16. 29–end	Lev. 25. 1, 8–17 Ps. 67 Matt. 14. 1–12	Ps. 20; 21; *23* Ezek. 24. 15–end James 1. 12–end
	Gr			
6	S	THE TRANSFIGURATION OF OUR LORD (*or* transferred to the 7th)		
			Dan. 7. 9–10, 13–14 Ps. 97 2 Pet. 1. 16–19	MP: Ps. 27; 150 Ecclus. 48. 1–10 *or* 1 Kings 19. 1–16
	ӝ		Luke 9. 28–36	1 John 3. 1–3
		or, for The Eighth Sunday after Trinity (Proper 13): *Track 1* Gen. 32. 22–31 Ps. 17. 1–7, 16 (*or* 17. 1–7) Rom. 9. 1–5 Matt. 14. 13–21	*Track 2* Isa. 55. 1–5 Ps. 145. 8–9, 15–end (*or* 145. 15–end) Rom. 9. 1–5	Ps. 85 Song of Sol. 5. 2–end *or* 1 Macc. 3. 1–12 2 Pet. 1. 1–15
	G		Matt. 14. 13–21	
7 DEL 18	M	For The Transfiguration of Our Lord, see the 6th. *John Mason Neale, Priest, Hymn Writer, 1866*	Num. 11. 4–15 Ps. 81. 11–end Matt. 14. 13–21	Ps. 27; *30* Ezek. 28. 1–19 James 2. 1–13
	G		(*or* 14. 22–end)	
8	Tu	**Dominic, Priest, Founder of the Order of Preachers, 1221**		
		Com. Religious *or* *also* Ecclus. 39. 1–10	Num. 12. 1–13 Ps. 51. 1–8 Matt. 14. 22–end	Ps. 32; *36* Ezek. 33. 1–20 James 2. 14–end
	Gw		*or* Matt. 15. 1–2, 10–14	
9	W	**Mary Sumner, Founder of the Mothers' Union, 1921**		
		Com. Saint *or* *also* Heb. 13. 1–5	Num. 13.1–2, 25 – 14.1, 26–35 Ps. 106. 14–24 Matt. 15. 21–28	Ps. 34 Ezek. 33. 21–end James ch. 3
	Gw			
10	Th	**Laurence, Deacon at Rome, Martyr, 258**		
		Com. Martyr *or* *also* 2 Cor. 9. 6–10	Num. 20. 1–13 Ps. 95. 1, 8–end Matt. 16. 13–23	Ps. 37† Ezek. 34. 1–16 James 4. 1–12
	Gr			
11	F	**Clare of Assisi, Founder of the Minoresses (Poor Clares), 1253**		
		John Henry Newman, Priest, Tractarian, 1890 Com. Religious *or* *esp.* Song of Sol. 8. 6–7	Deut. 4. 32–40 Ps. 77. 11–end Matt. 16. 24–end	Ps. 31 Ezek. 34. 17–end James 4.13 – 5.6
	Gw			
12	Sa		Deut. 6. 4–13 Ps. 18. 1–2, 48–end	Ps. 41; *42*; 43 Ezek. 36. 16–36
	G		Matt. 17. 14–20	James 5. 7–end

Second Service Evening Prayer		Calendar and Holy Communion	Morning Prayer	Evening Prayer
Ps. 18† I Sam. ch. 12 Luke 22. 47–62	G		Ezek. 20. 1–20 2 Cor. ch. 13	I Sam. ch. 12 Luke 22. 47–62
Ps. 22 I Sam. 13. 5–18 Luke 22. 63–end	G		Ezek. 20. 21–38 James 1. 1–11	I Sam. 13. 5–18 Luke 22. 63–end
Ps. *24*; 25 I Sam. 13.19 – 14.15 Luke 23. 1–12 **ct** *or First EP of The Transfiguration* Ps. 99; 110 Exod. 24. 12–end John 12. 27–36a 𝖂 **ct**	G		Ezek. 24. 15–end James 1. 12–end	I Sam. 13.19 – 14.15 Luke 23. 1–12 **ct** *or First EP of The Transfiguration* (Ps. 99; 110) Exod. 24. 12–end John 12. 27–36a 𝖂 **ct**
THE TRANSFIGURATION OF OUR LORD (or transferred to the 7th)				
EP: Ps. 72 Exod. 34. 29–end 2 Cor. ch. 3	𝖂	Exod. 24. 12–end Ps. 84. 1–7 1 John 3. 1–3 Mark 9. 2–7	Ps. 27; 150 Ecclus. 48. 1–10 *or* I Kings 19. 1–16 2 Pet. 1. 16–19	Ps. 72 Exod. 34. 29–end 2 Cor. ch. 3
		or, for the Eighth Sunday after Trinity:		
Ps. 80 (*or* 80. 1–8) I Kings 10. 1–13 Acts 13. 1–13 *Gospel:* John 6. 24–35	G	Jer. 23. 16–24 Ps. 31. 1–6 Rom. 8. 12–17 Matt. 7. 15–21	Ps. 85 Song of Sol. 5. 2–end *or* I Macc. 3. 1–12 2 Pet. 1. 1–15	Ps. 80 (*or* 80. 1–8) I Kings 10. 1–13 Acts 13. 1–13 *Gospel:* John 6. 24–35
		For the Transfiguration of Our Lord, see the 6th. **The Name of Jesus**		
Ps. 26; *28*; 29 I Sam. 14. 24–46 Luke 23. 13–25	Gw	Jer. 14. 7–9 Ps. 8 Acts 4. 8–12 Matt. 1. 20–23	Ezek. 28. 1–19 James 2. 1–13	I Sam. 14. 24–46 Luke 23. 13–25
Ps. 33 I Sam. 15. 1–23 Luke 23. 26–43	G		Ezek. 33. 1–20 James 2. 14–end	I Sam. 15. 1–23 Luke 23. 26–43
Ps. 119. 33–56 I Sam. ch. 16 Luke 23. 44–56a	G		Ezek. 33. 21–end James ch. 3	I Sam. ch. 16 Luke 23. 44–56a
Ps. 39; *40* I Sam. 17. 1–30 Luke 23.56b – 24.12	Gr	**Laurence, Deacon at Rome, Martyr, 258** Com. Martyr	Ezek. 34. 1–16 James 4. 1–12	I Sam. 17. 1–30 Luke 23.56b – 24.12
Ps. 35 I Sam. 17. 31–54 Luke 24. 13–35	G		Ezek. 34. 17–end James 4.13 – 5.6	I Sam. 17. 31–54 Luke 24. 13–35
Ps. 45; *46* I Sam. 17.55 – 18.16 Luke 24. 36–end **ct**	G		Ezek. 36. 16–36 James 5. 7–end	I Sam. 17.55 – 18.16 Luke 24. 36–end **ct**

August 2017

		Sunday Principal Service Weekday Eucharist	Third Service Morning Prayer
13	S G	THE NINTH SUNDAY AFTER TRINITY (**Proper 14**) *Track 1* Gen. 37. 1–4, 12–28 Ps. 105. 1–6, 16–22, 45b (*or* 105. 1–10) Rom. 10. 5–15 Matt. 14. 22–33	*Track 2* 1 Kings 19. 9–18 Ps. 85. 8–13 Rom. 10. 5–15 Matt. 14. 22–33	Ps. 88 Song of Sol. 8. 5–7 *or* 1 Macc. 14. 4–15 2 Pet. 3. 8–13
14 DEL 19	M G	*Maximilian Kolbe, Friar, Martyr, 1941*	Deut. 10. 12–end Ps. 147. 13–end Matt. 17. 22–end	Ps. 44 Ezek. 37. 1–14 Mark 1. 1–13
15	Tu W G	THE BLESSED VIRGIN MARY* *or, if The Blessed Virgin Mary is celebrated on 8 September:*	Isa. 61. 10–end *or* Rev. 11.19 – 12.6, 10 Ps. 45. 10–end Gal. 4. 4–7 Luke 1. 46–55 Deut. 31. 1–8 Ps. 107. 1–3, 42–end *or Canticle*: Deut. 32. 3–4, 7–9 Matt. 18. 1–5, 10, 12–14	MP: Ps. 98; 138; 147. 1–12 Isa. 7. 10–15 Luke 11. 27–28 Ps. **48**; 52 Ezek. 37. 15–end Mark 1. 14–20
16	W G		Deut. ch. 34 Ps. 66. 14–end Matt. 18. 15–20	Ps. 119. 57–80 Ezek. 39. 21–end Mark 1. 21–28
17	Th G		Josh. 3. 7–11, 13–17 Ps. 114 Matt. 18.21 – 19.1	Ps. 56; **57**; (63†) Ezek. 43. 1–12 Mark 1. 29–end
18	F G		Josh. 24. 1–13 Ps. 136. 1–3, 16–22 Matt. 19. 3–12	Ps. **51**; 54 Ezek. 44. 4–16 Mark 2. 1–12
19	Sa G		Josh. 24. 14–29 Ps. 16. 1, 5–end Matt. 19. 13–15	Ps. 68 Ezek. 47. 1–12 Mark 2. 13–22
20	S G	THE TENTH SUNDAY AFTER TRINITY (**Proper 15**) *Track 1* Gen. 45. 1–15 Ps. 133 Rom. 11. 1–2a, 29–32 Matt. 15. [10–20] 21–28	*Track 2* Isa. 56. 1, 6–8 Ps. 67 Rom. 11. 1–2a, 29–32 Matt. 15. [10–20] 21–28	Ps. 92 Jonah ch. 1 *or* Ecclus. 3. 1–15 2 Pet. 3. 14–end
21 DEL 20	M G		Judg. 2. 11–19 Ps. 106. 34–42 Matt. 19. 16–22	Ps. 71 Prov. 1. 1–19 Mark 2.23 – 3.6
22	Tu G		Judg. 6. 11–24 Ps. 85. 8–end Matt. 19. 23–end	Ps. 73 Prov. 1. 20–end Mark 3. 7–19a
23	W G		Judg. 9. 6–15 Ps. 21. 1–6 Matt. 20. 1–16	Ps. 77 Prov. ch. 2 Mark 3. 19b–end

*The Blessed Virgin Mary may be celebrated on 8 September instead of 15 August.

Second Service Evening Prayer		Calendar and Holy Communion	Morning Prayer	Evening Prayer
		THE NINTH SUNDAY AFTER TRINITY		
Ps. 86 I Kings 11.41 – 12.20 Acts 14. 8–20 *Gospel*: John 6. 35, 41–51	G	Num. 10.35 – 11.3 Ps. 95 I Cor. 10. 1–13 Luke 16. 1–9 *or* Luke 15. 11–end	Ps. 88 Song of Sol. 8. 5–7 *or* I Macc. 14. 4–15 2 Pet. 3. 8–13	Ps. 86 I Kings 11.41 – 12.20 Acts 14. 8–20
Ps. **47**; 49 I Sam. 19. 1–18 Acts 1. 1–14 *or First EP of The Blessed Virgin Mary* Ps. 72 Prov. 8. 22–31 John 19. 23–27 **W ct**	G		Ezek. 37. 1–14 Mark 1. 1–13	I Sam. 19. 1–18 Acts 1. 1–14
EP: Ps. 132 Song of Sol. 2. 1–7 Acts 1. 6–14		To celebrate The Blessed Virgin Mary, see *Common Worship* provision. Ezek. 37. 15–end Mark 1. 14–20		I Sam. 20. 1–17 Acts 1. 15–end
Ps. 50 I Sam. 20. 1–17 Acts 1. 15–end	G			
Ps. **59**; 60; (67) I Sam. 20. 18–end Acts 2. 1–21	G		Ezek. 39. 21–end Mark 1. 21–28	I Sam. 20. 18–end Acts 2. 1–21
Ps. 61; **62**; 64 I Sam. 21.1 – 22.5 Acts 2. 22–36	G		Ezek. 43. 1–12 Mark 1. 29–end	I Sam. 21.1 – 22.5 Acts 2. 22–36
Ps. 38 I Sam. 22. 6–end Acts 2. 37–end	G		Ezek. 44. 4–16 Mark 2. 1–12	I Sam. 22. 6–end Acts 2. 37–end
Ps. 65; **66** I Sam. ch. 23 Acts 3. 1–10 **ct**	G		Ezek. 47. 1–12 Mark 2. 13–22	I Sam. ch. 23 Acts 3. 1–10 **ct**
		THE TENTH SUNDAY AFTER TRINITY		
Ps. 90 (*or* 90. 1–12) 2 Kings 4. 1–37 Acts 16. 1–15 *Gospel*: John 6. 51–58	G	Jer. 7. 9–15 Ps. 17. 1–8 I Cor. 12. 1–11 Luke 19. 41–47a	Ps. 92 Jonah ch. 1 *or* Ecclus. 3. 1–15 2 Pet. 3. 14–end	Ps. 90 (*or* 90. 1–12) 2 Kings 4. 1–37 Acts 16. 1–15
Ps. **72**; 75 I Sam. ch. 24 Acts 3. 11–end	G		Prov. 1. 1–19 Mark 2.23 – 3.6	I Sam. ch. 24 Acts 3. 11–end
Ps. 74 I Sam. ch. 26 Acts 4. 1–12	G		Prov. 1. 20–end Mark 3. 7–19a	I Sam. ch. 26 Acts 4. 1–12
Ps. 119. 81–104 I Sam. 28. 3–end Acts 4. 13–31 *or First EP of Bartholomew* Ps. 97 Isa. 61. 1–9 2 Cor. 6. 1–10 **R ct**	G		Prov. ch. 2 Mark 3. 19b–end	I Sam. 28. 3–end Acts 4. 13–31 *or First EP of Bartholomew* (Ps. 97) Isa. 61. 1–9 2 Cor. 6. 1–10 **R ct**

August 2017

			Sunday Principal Service / Weekday Eucharist	Third Service / Morning Prayer

August 2017

24	Th	**BARTHOLOMEW THE APOSTLE**	Isa. 43. 8–13 / or Acts 5. 12–16 / Ps. 145. 1–7 / Acts 5. 12–16 / or 1 Cor. 4. 9–15 / Luke 22. 24–30	*MP*: Ps. 86; 117 / Gen. 28. 10–17 / John 1. 43–end
	R			
25	F		Ruth 1. 1, 3–6, 14–16, 22 / Ps. 146 / Matt. 22. 34–40	Ps. 55 / Prov. 3.27 – 4.19 / Mark 4. 21–34
	G			
26	Sa		Ruth 2. 1–3, 8–11; 4. 13–17 / Ps. 128 / Matt. 23. 1–12	Ps. **76**; 79 / Prov. 6. 1–19 / Mark 4. 35–end
	G			

27	S	**THE ELEVENTH SUNDAY AFTER TRINITY (Proper 16)**	*Track 1*		

		Track 1	*Track 2*	
27 S		Exod. 1.8 – 2.10	Isa. 51. 1–6	Ps. 104. 1–25
		Ps. 124	Ps. 138	Jonah ch. 2
		Rom. 12. 1–8	Rom. 12. 1–8	or Ecclus. 3. 17–29
	G	Matt. 16. 13–20	Matt. 16. 13–20	Rev. ch. 1
28 DEL 21	M	**Augustine, Bishop of Hippo, Teacher, 430** / Com. Teacher *or* / *esp.* Ecclus. 39. 1–10 / *also* Rom. 13. 11–13	1 Thess. 1. 1–5, 8–end / Ps. 149. 1–5 / Matt. 23. 13–22	Ps. **80**; 82 / Prov. 8. 1–21 / Mark 5. 1–20
	Gw			
29	Tu	**The Beheading of John the Baptist** / Jer. 1. 4–10 *or* / Ps. 11 / Heb. 11.32 – 12.2 / Matt. 14. 1–12	1 Thess. 2. 1–8 / Ps. 139. 1–9 / Matt. 23. 23–26	Ps. 87; **89. 1–18** / Prov. 8. 22–end / Mark 5. 21–34
	Gr			
30	W	**John Bunyan, Spiritual Writer, 1688** / Com. Teacher *or* / *also* Heb. 12. 1–2 / Luke 21. 21, 34–36	1 Thess. 2. 9–13 / Ps. 126 / Matt. 23. 27–32	Ps. 119. 105–128 / Prov. ch. 9 / Mark 5. 35–end
	Gw			
31	Th	**Aidan, Bishop of Lindisfarne, Missionary, 651** / Com. Missionary *or* / *also* 1 Cor. 9. 16–19	1 Thess. 3. 7–end / Ps. 90. 13–end / Matt. 24. 42–end	Ps. 90; **92** / Prov. 10. 1–12 / Mark 6. 1–13
	Gw			

September 2017

1	F	*Giles of Provence, Hermit, c. 710*	1 Thess. 4. 1–8 / Ps. 97 / Matt. 25. 1–13	Ps. **88**; (95) / Prov. 11. 1–12 / Mark 6. 14–29
	G			
2	Sa	*The Martyrs of Papua New Guinea, 1901 and 1942*	1 Thess. 4. 9–12 / Ps. 98. 1–2, 8–end / Matt. 25. 14–30	Ps. 96; **97**; 100 / Prov. 12. 10–end / Mark 6. 30–44
	G			

3	S	**THE TWELFTH SUNDAY AFTER TRINITY (Proper 17)**			

		Track 1	*Track 2*	
3 S		Exod. 3. 1–15	Jer. 15. 15–21	Ps. 107. 1–32
		Ps. 105. 1–6, 23–26, 45b	Ps. 26. 1–8	Jonah 3. 1–9
		or Ps. 115	Rom. 12. 9–end	or Ecclus. 11. [7–18] 19–28
		Rom. 12. 9–end	Matt. 16. 21–end	Rev. 3. 14–end
	G	Matt. 16. 21–end		
4 DEL 22	M	*Birinus, Bishop of Dorchester (Oxon), Apostle of Wessex, 650**	1 Thess. 4. 13–end / Ps. 96 / Luke 4. 16–30	Ps. **98**; 99; 101 / Prov. 14.31 – 15.17 / Mark 6. 45–end
	G			

*Cuthbert may be celebrated on 4 September instead of 20 March.

Second Service Evening Prayer		Calendar and Holy Communion	Morning Prayer	Evening Prayer
EP: Ps. 91; 116 Ecclus. 39. 1–10 *or* Deut. 18. 15–19 Matt. 10. 1–22	R	**BARTHOLOMEW THE APOSTLE** Gen. 28. 10–17 Ps. 15 Acts 5. 12–16 Luke 22. 24–30	(Ps. 86; 117) Isa. 43. 8–13 John 1. 43–end	(Ps. 91; 116) Ecclus. 39. 1–10 *or* Deut. 18. 15–19 Matt. 10. 1–22
Ps. 69 2 Sam. ch. 1 Acts 5. 12–26	G		Prov. 3.27 – 4.19 Mark 4. 21–34	2 Sam. ch. 1 Acts 5. 12–26
Ps. 81; *84* 2 Sam. 2. 1–11 Acts 5. 27–end ct	G		Prov. 6. 1–19 Mark 4. 35–end	2 Sam. 2. 1–11 Acts 5. 27–end ct
Ps. 95 2 Kings 6. 8–23 Acts 17. 15–end *Gospel*: John 6. 56–69	G	**THE ELEVENTH SUNDAY AFTER TRINITY** 1 Kings 3. 5–15 Ps. 28 1 Cor. 15. 1–11 Luke 18. 9–14	Ps. 104. 1–25 Jonah ch. 2 *or* Ecclus. 3. 17–29 Rev. ch. 1	Ps. 95 2 Kings 6. 8–23 Acts 17. 15–end
Ps. *85*; 86 2 Sam. 3. 12–end Acts ch. 6	Gw	**Augustine, Bishop of Hippo, 430** Com. Doctor	Prov. 8. 1–21 Mark 5. 1–20	2 Sam. 3. 12–end Acts ch. 6
Ps. 89. 19–end 2 Sam. 5. 1–12 Acts 7. 1–16	Gr	**The Beheading of John the Baptist** 2 Chron. 24. 17–21 Ps. 92. 11–end Heb. 11.32 – 12.2 Matt. 14. 1–12	Prov. 8. 22–end Mark 5. 21–34	2 Sam. 5. 1–12 Acts 7. 1–16
Ps. *91*; 93 2 Sam. 6. 1–19 Acts 7. 17–43	G		Prov. ch. 9 Mark 5. 35–end	2 Sam. 6. 1–19 Acts 7. 17–43
Ps. 94 2 Sam. 7. 1–17 Acts 7. 44–53	G		Prov. 10. 1–12 Mark 6. 1–13	2 Sam. 7. 1–17 Acts 7. 44–53
Ps. 102 2 Sam. 7. 18–end Acts 7.54 – 8.3	Gw	**Giles of Provence, Hermit, c. 710** Com. Abbot	Prov. 11. 1–12 Mark 6. 14–29	2 Sam. 7. 18–end Acts 7.54 – 8.3
Ps. 104 2 Sam. ch. 9 Acts 8. 4–25 ct	G		Prov. 12. 10–end Mark 6. 30–44	2 Sam. ch. 9 Acts 8. 4–25 ct
Ps. 105. 1–15 2 Kings 6. 24–25; 7. 3–end Acts 18. 1–16 *Gospel*: Mark 7. 1–8, 14–15, 21–23	G	**THE TWELFTH SUNDAY AFTER TRINITY** Exod. 34. 29–end Ps. 34. 1–10 2 Cor. 3. 4–9 Mark 7. 31–37	Ps. 107. 1–32 Jonah 3. 1–9 *or* Ecclus. 11. [7–18] 19–28 Rev. 3. 14–end	Ps. 105. 1–15 2 Kings 6. 24–25; 7. 3–end Acts 18. 1–16
Ps. *105*† (*or* 103) 2 Sam. ch. 11 Acts 8. 26–end	G		Prov. 14.31 – 15.17 Mark 6. 45–end	2 Sam. ch. 11 Acts 8. 26–end

September 2017

			Sunday Principal Service Weekday Eucharist	Third Service Morning Prayer
5	Tu G		I Thess. 5. 1–6, 9–11 Ps. 27. 1–8 Luke 4. 31–37	Ps. *106*† (or 103) Prov. 15. 18–end Mark 7. 1–13
6	W G	*Allen Gardiner, Missionary, Founder of the South American Mission Society, 1851* Col. 1. 1–8 Ps. 34. 11–18 Luke 4. 38–end	Ps. 110; *111*; 112 Prov. 18. 10–end Mark 7. 14–23
7	Th G		Col. 1. 9–14 Ps. 98. 1–5 Luke 5. 1–11	Ps. 113; *115* Prov. 20. 1–22 Mark 7. 24–30
8	F Gw	**The Birth of the Blessed Virgin Mary*** Com. BVM	*or* Col. 1. 15–20 Ps. 89. 19b–28 Luke 5. 33–end	Ps. 139 Prov. 22. 1–16 Mark 7. 31–end
9	Sa G	*Charles Fuge Lowder, Priest, 1880*	Col. 1. 21–23 Ps. 117 Luke 6. 1–5	Ps. 120; *121*; 122 Prov. 24. 23–end Mark 8. 1–10
10	S G	THE THIRTEENTH SUNDAY AFTER TRINITY (**Proper 18**) *Track 1* Exod. 12. 1–14 Ps. 149 Rom. 13. 8–end Matt. 18. 15–20	*Track 2* Ezek. 33. 7–11 Ps. 119. 33–40 Rom. 13. 8–end Matt. 18. 15–20	Ps. 119. 17–32 Jonah 3.10 – 4.11 or Ecclus. 27.30 – 28.9 Rev. 8. 1–5
11 DEL 23	M G		Col. 1.24 – 2.3 Ps. 62. 1–7 Luke 6. 6–11	Ps. 123; 124; 125; *126* Prov. 25. 1–14 Mark 8. 11–21
12	Tu G		Col. 2. 6–15 Ps. 8 Luke 6. 12–19	Ps. *132*; 133 Prov. 25. 15–end Mark 8. 22–26
13	W Gw	**John Chrysostom, Bishop of Constantinople, Teacher, 407** Com. Teacher *esp.* Matt. 5. 13–19 *also* Jer. 1. 4–10	*or* Col. 3. 1–11 Ps. 15 Luke 6. 20–26	Ps. 119. 153–end Prov. 26. 12–end Mark 8.27 – 9.1
14	Th R	HOLY CROSS DAY	Num. 21. 4–9 Ps. 22. 23–28 Phil. 2. 6–11 John 3. 13–17	MP: Ps. 2; 8; 146 Gen. 3. 1–15 John 12. 27–36a
15	F Gr	**Cyprian, Bishop of Carthage, Martyr, 258** Com. Martyr *esp.* 1 Pet. 4. 12–end *also* Matt. 18. 18–22	*or* 1 Tim. 1. 1–2, 12–14 Ps. 16 Luke 6. 39–42	Ps. 142; *144* Prov. 30. 1–9, 24–31 Mark 9. 14–29
16	Sa Gw	**Ninian, Bishop of Galloway, Apostle of the Picts, c. 432** *Edward Bouverie Pusey, Priest, Tractarian, 1882* Com. Missionary *esp.* Acts 13. 46–49 Mark 16. 15–end	*or* 1 Tim. 1. 15–17 Ps. 113 Luke 6. 43–end	Ps. 147 Prov. 31. 10–end Mark 9. 30–37

*The Blessed Virgin Mary may be celebrated on 8 September instead of 15 August.

Second Service Evening Prayer		Calendar and Holy Communion	Morning Prayer	Evening Prayer
Ps. 107† 2 Sam. 12. 1–25 Acts 9. 1–19a	G		Prov. 15. 18–end Mark 7. 1–13	2 Sam. 12. 1–25 Acts 9. 1–19a
Ps. 119. 129–152 2 Sam. 15. 1–12 Acts 9. 19b–31	G		Prov. 18. 10–end Mark 7. 14–23	2 Sam. 15. 1–12 Acts 9. 19b–31
Ps. 114; *116*; 117 2 Sam. 15. 13–end Acts 9. 32–end	Gw	**Evurtius, Bishop of Orleans, 4th century** Com. Bishop	Prov. 20. 1–22 Mark 7. 24–30	2 Sam. 15. 13–end Acts 9. 32–end
Ps. *130*; 131; 137 2 Sam. 16. 1–14 Acts 10. 1–16	Gw	**The Nativity of the Blessed Virgin Mary** Gen. 3. 9–15 Ps. 45. 11–18 Rom. 5. 12–17 Luke 11. 27–28	Prov. 22. 1–16 Mark 7. 31–end	2 Sam. 16. 1–14 Acts 10. 1–16
Ps. 118 2 Sam. 17. 1–23 Acts 10. 17–33 ct	G		Prov. 24. 23–end Mark 8. 1–10	2 Sam. 17. 1–23 Acts 10. 17–33 ct
Ps. 108; [115] Ezek. 12.21 – 13.16 Acts 19. 1–20 *Gospel:* Mark 7. 24–end	G	THE THIRTEENTH SUNDAY AFTER TRINITY Lev. 19. 13–18 Ps. 74. 20–end Gal. 3. 16–22 *or* Heb. 13. 1–6 Luke 10. 23b–37	Ps. 119. 17–32 Jonah 3.10 – 4.11 *or* Ecclus. 27.30 – 28.9 Rev. 8. 1–5	Ps. 108; [115] Ezek. 12.21 – 13.16 Mark 7. 24–30
Ps. *127*; 128; 129 2 Sam. 18. 1–18 Acts 10. 34–end	G		Prov. 25. 1–14 Mark 8. 11–21	2 Sam. 18. 1–18 Acts 10. 34–end
Ps. (134); *135* 2 Sam. 18.19 – 19.8a Acts 11. 1–18	G		Prov. 25. 15–end Mark 8. 22–26	2 Sam. 18.19 – 19.8a Acts 11. 1–18
Ps. 136 2 Sam. 19. 8b–23 Acts 11. 19–end *or First EP of Holy Cross Day* Ps. 66 Isa. 52.13 – 53.end Eph. 2. 11–end **R** ct	G		Prov. 26. 12–end Mark 8.27 – 9.1	2 Sam. 19. 8b–23 Acts 11. 19–end
EP: Ps. 110; 150 Isa. 63. 1–16 1 Cor. 1. 18–25	Gr	**Holy Cross Day** To celebrate Holy Cross as a festival, see *Common Worship* provision. Num. 21. 4–9 Ps. 67 1 Cor. 1. 17–25 John 12. 27–33	Prov. 27. 1–22 Mark 9. 2–13	2 Sam. 19. 24–end Acts 12. 1–17
Ps. 145 2 Sam. 23. 1–7 Acts 12. 18–end	G		Prov. 30. 1–9, 24–31 Mark 9. 14–29	2 Sam. 23. 1–7 Acts 12. 18–end
Ps. *148*; 149; 150 2 Sam. ch. 24 Acts 13. 1–12 ct	G		Prov. 31. 10–end Mark 9. 30–37	2 Sam. ch. 24 Acts 13. 1–12 ct

September 2017

		Sunday Principal Service / Weekday Eucharist		Third Service / Morning Prayer

17 S — THE FOURTEENTH SUNDAY AFTER TRINITY (Proper 19)

Track 1
Exod. 14. 19–end
Ps. 114
or Canticle: Exod. 15. 1b–11, 20–21
Rom. 14. 1–12
G Matt. 18. 21–35

Track 2
Gen. 50. 15–21
Ps. 103. 1–13 (or 103. 8–13)
Rom. 14. 1–12
Matt. 18. 21–35

Ps. 119. 65–88
Isa. 44.24 – 45.8
Rev. 12. 1–12

18 M
DEL 24
G
1 Tim. 2. 1–8
Ps. 28
Luke 7. 1–10

Ps. 1; 2; 3
Wisd. ch. 1
or 1 Chron. 10.1 – 11.9
Mark 9. 38–end

19 Tu Theodore of Tarsus, Archbishop of Canterbury, 690
1 Tim. 3. 1–13
Ps. 101
Luke 7. 11–17
G

Ps. 5; 6; (8)
Wisd. ch. 2
or 1 Chron. ch. 13
Mark 10. 1–16

20 W John Coleridge Patteson, first Bishop of Melanesia and his Companions, Martyrs, 1871
Com. Martyr   or
esp. 2 Chron. 24. 17–21
also Acts 7. 55–end

1 Tim. 3. 14–end
Ps. 111. 1–5
Luke 7. 31–35

Ps. 119. 1–32
Wisd. 3. 1–9
or 1 Chron. 15.1 – 16.3
Mark 10. 17–31

Gr

21 Th MATTHEW, APOSTLE AND EVANGELIST
R
Prov. 3. 13–18
Ps. 119. 65–72
2 Cor. 4. 1–6
Matt. 9. 9–13

MP: Ps. 49; 117
1 Kings 19. 15–end
2 Tim. 3. 14–end

22 F
G
1 Tim. 6. 2b–12
Ps. 49. 1–9
Luke 8. 1–3

Ps. 17; 19
Wisd. 5. 1–16
or 1 Chron. 21.1 – 22.1
Mark 10. 35–45

23 Sa
G
1 Tim. 6. 13–16
Ps. 100
Luke 8. 4–15

Ps. 20; 21; 23
Wisd. 5.17 – 6.11
or 1 Chron. 22. 2–end
Mark 10. 46–end

24 S — THE FIFTEENTH SUNDAY AFTER TRINITY (Proper 20)

Track 1
Exod. 16. 2–15
Ps. 105. 1–6, 37–end
(or 105. 37–end)
Phil. 1. 21–end
G Matt. 20. 1–16

Track 2
Jonah 3.10 – 4.end
Ps. 145. 1–8
Phil. 1. 21–end
Matt. 20. 1–16

Ps. 119. 153–end
Isa. 45. 9–22
Rev. 14. 1–5

25 M Lancelot Andrewes, Bishop of Winchester, Spiritual Writer, 1626
DEL 25
Sergei of Radonezh, Russian Monastic Reformer, Teacher, 1392
Com. Bishop   or
esp. Isa. 6. 1–8
Gw

Ezra 1. 1–6
Ps. 126
Luke 8. 16–18

Ps. 27; 30
Wisd. 6. 12–23
or 1 Chron. 28. 1–10
Mark 11. 1–11

26 Tu Wilson Carlile, Founder of the Church Army, 1942
G
Ezra 6. 7–8, 12, 14–20
Ps. 124
Luke 8. 19–21

Ps. 32; 36
Wisd. 7. 1–14
or 1 Chron. 28. 11–end
Mark 11. 12–26

27 W Vincent de Paul, Founder of the Congregation of the Mission (Lazarists), 1660
Ember Day*
Com. Religious   or
also 1 Cor. 1. 25–end
Matt. 25. 34–40
Gw or Rw

Ezra 9. 5–9
Canticle: Song of Tobit
or Ps. 103. 1–6
Luke 9. 1–6

Ps. 34
Wisd. 7.15 – 8.4
or 1 Chron. 29. 1–9
Mark 11. 27–end

*For Ember Day provision, see p. 11.

Second Service Evening Prayer	Calendar and Holy Communion		Morning Prayer	Evening Prayer
	THE FOURTEENTH SUNDAY AFTER TRINITY			
Ps. 119. 41–48 [49–64] Ezek. 20. 1–8, 33–44 Acts 20. 17–end *Gospel*: Mark 8. 27–end	2 Kings 5. 9–16 Ps. 118. 1–9 Gal. 5. 16–24 Luke 17. 11–19	G	Ps. 119. 65–88 Isa. 44.24 – 45.8 Rev. 12. 1–12	Ps. 119. 41–48 [49–64] Ezek. 20. 1–8, 33–44 Acts 20. 17–end
Ps. *4*; 7 1 Kings 1. 5–31 Acts 13. 13–43		G	Wisd. ch. 1 *or* 1 Chron. 10.1 – 11.9 Mark 9. 38–end	1 Kings 1. 5–31 Acts 13. 13–43
Ps. *9*; 10† 1 Kings 1.32 – 2.4, 10–12 Acts 13.44 – 14.7		G	Wisd. ch. 2 *or* 1 Chron. ch. 13 Mark 10. 1–16	1 Kings 1.32 – 2.4, 10–12 Acts 13.44 – 14.7
Ps. *11*; 12; 13 1 Kings ch. 3 Acts 14. 8–end *or First EP of Matthew* Ps. 34 Isa. 33. 13–17 Matt. 6. 19–end **R ct**		G	Wisd. 3. 1–9 *or* 1 Chron. 15.1 – 16.3 Mark 10. 17–31	1 Kings ch. 3 Acts 14. 8–end *or First EP of Matthew* (Ps. 34) Prov. 3. 3–18 Matt. 6. 19–end **R ct**
	MATTHEW, APOSTLE AND EVANGELIST			
EP: Ps. 119. 33–40, 89–96 Eccles. 5. 4–12 Matt. 19. 16–end	Isa. 33. 13–17 Ps. 119. 65–72 2 Cor. 4. 1–6 Matt. 9. 9–13	R	(Ps. 49; 117) 1 Kings 19. 15–end 2 Tim. 3. 14–end	(Ps. 119. 33–40, 89–96) Eccles. 5. 4–12 Matt. 19. 16–end
Ps. 22 1 Kings 6. 1, 11–28 Acts 15. 22–35		G	Wisd. 5. 1–16 *or* 1 Chron. 21.1 – 22.1 Mark 10. 35–45	1 Kings 6. 1, 11–28 Acts 15. 22–35
Ps. *24*; 25 1 Kings 8. 1–30 Acts 15.36 – 16.5 **ct**		G	Wisd. 5.17 – 6.11 *or* 1 Chron. 22. 2–end Mark 10. 46–end	1 Kings 8. 1–30 Acts 15.36 – 16.5 **ct**
	THE FIFTEENTH SUNDAY AFTER TRINITY			
Ps. 119. 113–136 (*or* 119. 121–128) Ezek. 33.23, 30 – 34.10 Acts 26. 1, 9–25 *Gospel*: Mark 9. 30–37	Josh. 24. 14–25 Ps. 92. 1–6 Gal. 6. 11–end Matt. 6. 24–end	G	Ps. 119. 153–end Isa. 45. 9–22 Rev. 14. 1–5	Ps. 119. 113–136 (*or* 119. 121–128) Ezek. 33.23, 30 – 34.10 Acts 26. 1, 9–25
Ps. 26; *28*; 29 1 Kings 8. 31–62 Acts 16. 6–24		G	Wisd. 6. 12–23 *or* 1 Chron. 28. 1–10 Mark 11. 1–11	1 Kings 8. 31–62 Acts 16. 6–24
Ps. 33 1 Kings 8.63 – 9.9 Acts 16. 25–end	**Cyprian, Bishop of Carthage, Martyr, 258** Com. Martyr	Gr	Wisd. 7. 1–14 *or* 1 Chron. 28. 11–end Mark 11. 12–26	1 Kings 8.63 – 9.9 Acts 16. 25–end
Ps. 119. 33–56 1 Kings 10. 1–25 Acts 17. 1–15	Ember Day Ember CEG	G *or* R	Wisd. 7.15 – 8.4 *or* 1 Chron. 29. 1–9 Mark 11. 27–end	1 Kings 10. 1–25 Acts 17. 1–15

September 2017

			Sunday Principal Service Weekday Eucharist	Third Service Morning Prayer
28	Th		Hag. 1. 1–8 Ps. 149. 1–5 Luke 9. 7–9	Ps. 37† Wisd. 8. 5–18 *or* 1 Chron. 29. 10–20 Mark 12. 1–12
	G			
29	F	MICHAEL AND ALL ANGELS Ember Day*	Gen. 28. 10–17 *or* Rev. 12. 7–12 Ps. 103. 19–end Rev. 12. 7–12 *or* Heb. 1. 5–end John 1. 47–end	*MP*: Ps. 34; 150 Tobit 12. 6–end *or* Dan. 12. 1–4 Acts 12. 1–11
	W			
30	Sa	Ember Day* *Jerome, Translator of the Scriptures, Teacher, 420*	Zech. 2. 1–5, 10–11 Ps. 125 *or Canticle*: Jer. 31. 10–13 Luke 9. 43b–45	Ps. 41; **42**; 43 Wisd. 10.15 – 11.10 *or* 2 Chron. 1. 1–13 Mark 12. 18–27
	G *or* **R**			

October 2017

1	S	THE SIXTEENTH SUNDAY AFTER TRINITY **(Proper 21)** *Track 1* Exod. 17. 1–7 Ps. 78. 1–4, 12–16 (*or* 78. 1–7) Phil. 2. 1–13 Matt. 21. 23–32	*Track 2* Ezek. 18. 1–4, 25–end Ps. 25. 1–8 Phil. 2. 1–13 Matt. 21. 23–32	Ps. 125; 126; 127 Isa. 48. 12–21 Luke 11. 37–54
	G			
			or, if observed as Dedication Festival: 1 Kings 8. 22–30 *or* Rev. 21. 9–14 Ps. 122 Heb. 12. 18–24 Matt. 21. 12–16	*MP*: Ps. 48; 150 Hag. 2. 6–9 Heb. 10. 19–25
	⅏			
2 DEL 26	M		Zech. 8. 1–8 Ps. 102. 12–22 Luke 9. 46–50	Ps. 44 Wisd. 11.21 – 12.2 *or* 2 Chron. 2. 1–16 Mark 12. 28–34
	G			
3	Tu	*George Bell, Bishop of Chichester, Ecumenist, Peacemaker, 1958*	Zech. 8. 20–end Ps. 87 Luke 9. 51–56	Ps. **48**; 52 Wisd. 12. 12–21 *or* 2 Chron. ch. 3 Mark 12. 35–end
	G			
4	W	**Francis of Assisi, Friar, Deacon, Founder of the Friars Minor, 1226** Com. Religious *or* *also* Gal. 6. 14–end Luke 12. 22–34	Neh. 2. 1–8 Ps. 137. 1–6 Luke 9. 57–end	Ps. 119. 57–80 Wisd. 13. 1–9 *or* 2 Chron. ch. 5 Mark 13. 1–13
	Gw			
5	Th		Neh. 8. 1–12 Ps. 19. 7–11 Luke 10. 1–12	Ps. 56; **57**; (63†) Wisd. 16.15 – 17.1 *or* 2 Chron. 6. 1–21 Mark 13. 14–23
	G			

*For Ember Day provision, see p. 11.

Second Service / Evening Prayer	Calendar and Holy Communion	Morning Prayer	Evening Prayer
Ps. 39; *40* 1 Kings 11. 1–13 Acts 17. 16–end *or First EP of Michael and All Angels* Ps. 91 2 Kings 6. 8–17 Matt. 18. 1–6, 10 **W ct**	G	Wisd. 8. 5–18 *or* 1 Chron. 29. 10–20 Mark 12. 1–12	1 Kings 11. 1–13 Acts 17. 16–end *or First EP of Michael and All Angels* (Ps. 91) 2 Kings 6. 8–17 John 1. 47–51 **W ct**
EP: Ps. 138; 148 Dan. 10. 4–end Rev. ch. 5	**MICHAEL AND ALL ANGELS** Ember Day Dan. 10. 10–19a Ps. 103. 17–22 Rev. 12. 7–12 Matt. 18. 1–10 W	(Ps. 34; 150) Tobit 12. 6–end *or* Dan. 12. 1–4 Acts 12. 1–11	(Ps. 138; 148) Gen. 28. 10–17 Rev. ch. 5
Ps. 45; *46* 1 Kings 12. 1–24 Acts 18.22 – 19.7 **ct** *or First EP of Dedication Festival* Ps. 24 2 Chron. 7. 11–16 John 4. 19–29 ₩ **ct**	**Jerome, Translator of the Scriptures, Teacher, 420** Ember Day Ember CEG Com. Doctor Gw	Wisd. 10.15 – 11.10 *or* 2 Chron. 1. 1–13 Mark 12. 18–27	1 Kings 12. 1–24 Acts 18.22 – 19.7 **ct** *or First EP of Dedication Festival* Ps. 24 2 Chron. 7. 11–16 John 4. 19–29 ₩ **ct**
Ps. [120; 123]; 124 Ezek. 37. 15–end 1 John 2. 22–end *Gospel*: Mark 9. 38–end	**THE SIXTEENTH SUNDAY AFTER TRINITY** G 1 Kings 17. 17–end Ps. 102. 12–17 Eph. 3. 13–end Luke 7. 11–17	Ps. 125; 126; 127 Isa. 48. 12–21 Luke 11. 37–54	Ps. [120; 123]; 124 Ezek. 37. 15–end 1 John 2. 22–end
EP: Ps. 132 Jer. 7. 1–11 1 Cor. 3. 9–17 *Gospel*: Luke 19. 1–10	*or, if observed as Dedication Festival*: 2 Chron. 7. 11–16 Ps. 122 1 Cor. 3. 9–17 *or* 1 Pet. 2. 1–5 Matt. 21. 12–16 ₩ *or* John 10. 22–29	Ps. 48; 150 Hag. 2. 6–9 Heb. 10. 19–25	Ps. 132 Jer. 7. 1–11 Luke 19. 1–10
Ps. *47*; 49 1 Kings 12.25 – 13.10 Acts 19. 8–20	G	Wisd. 11.21 – 12.2 *or* 2 Chron. 2. 1–16 Mark 12. 28–34	1 Kings 12.25 – 13.10 Acts 19. 8–20
Ps. 50 1 Kings 13. 11–end Acts 19. 21–end	G	Wisd. 12. 12–21 *or* 2 Chron. ch. 3 Mark 12. 35–end	1 Kings 13. 11–end Acts 19. 21–end
Ps. *59*; 60; (67) 1 Kings ch. 17 Acts 20. 1–16	G	Wisd. 13. 1–9 *or* 2 Chron. ch. 5 Mark 13. 1–13	1 Kings ch. 17 Acts 20. 1–16
Ps. 61; *62*; 64 1 Kings 18. 1–20 Acts 20. 17–end	G	Wisd. 16.15 – 17.1 *or* 2 Chron. 6. 1–21 Mark 13. 14–23	1 Kings 18. 1–20 Acts 20. 17–end

October 2017

			Sunday Principal Service / Weekday Eucharist	Third Service / Morning Prayer
6	F / Gr	**William Tyndale, Translator of the Scriptures, Reformation Martyr, 1536** Com. Martyr *also* Prov. 8. 4–11 2 Tim. 3. 12–end	*or* Baruch 1. 15–end *or* Deut. 31. 7–13 Ps. 79. 1–9 Luke 10. 13–16	Ps. *51*; 54 Wisd. 18. 6–19 or 2 Chron. 6. 22–end Mark 13. 24–31
7	Sa / G		Baruch 4. 5–12, 27–29 or Josh. 22. 1–6 Ps. 69. 33–37 Luke 10. 17–24	Ps. 68 Wisd. ch. 19 or 2 Chron. ch. 7 Mark 13. 32–end
8	S / G	**THE SEVENTEENTH SUNDAY AFTER TRINITY (Proper 22)** *Track 1* Exod. 20. 1–4, 7–9, 12–20 Ps. 19 (or 19. 7–end) Phil. 3. 4b–14 Matt. 21. 33–end	*Track 2* Isa. 5. 1–7 Ps. 80. 9–17 Phil. 3. 4b–14 Matt. 21. 33–end	Ps. 128; 129; 134 Isa. 49. 13–23 Luke 12. 1–12
9 DEL 27	M / G	*Denys, Bishop of Paris, and his Companions, Martyrs, c. 250; Robert Grosseteste, Bishop of Lincoln, Philosopher, Scientist, 1253*	Jonah 1.1 – 2.2, 10 Canticle: Jonah 2. 2–4, 7 or Ps. 69. 1–6 Luke 10. 25–37	Ps. 71 1 Macc. 1. 1–19 or 2 Chron. 9. 1–12 Mark 14. 1–11
10	Tu / Gw	**Paulinus, Bishop of York, Missionary, 644** *Thomas Traherne, Poet, Spiritual Writer, 1674* Com. Missionary *esp.* Matt. 28. 16–end	*or* Jonah ch. 3 Ps. 130 Luke 10. 38–end	Ps. 73 1 Macc. 1. 20–40 or 2 Chron. 10.1 – 11.4 Mark 14. 12–25
11	W / G	*Ethelburga, Abbess of Barking, 675; James the Deacon, Companion of Paulinus, 7th century*	Jonah ch. 4 Ps. 86. 1–9 Luke 11. 1–4	Ps. 77 1 Macc. 1. 41–end or 2 Chron. ch. 12 Mark 14. 26–42
12	Th / Gw	**Wilfrid of Ripon, Bishop, Missionary, 709** *Elizabeth Fry, Prison Reformer, 1845; Edith Cavell, Nurse, 1915* Com. Missionary *esp.* Luke 5. 1–11 *also* 1 Cor. 1. 18–25	*or* Mal. 3.13 – 4.2a Ps. 1 Luke 11. 5–13	Ps. 78. 1–39† 1 Macc. 2. 1–28 or 2 Chron. 13.1 – 14.1 Mark 14. 43–52
13	F / Gw	**Edward the Confessor, King of England, 1066** Com. Saint *also* 2 Sam. 23. 1–5 1 John 4. 13–16	*or* Joel 1. 13–15; 2. 1–2 Ps. 9. 1–7 Luke 11. 15–26	Ps. 55 1 Macc. 2. 29–48 or 2 Chron. 14. 2–end Mark 14. 53–65
14	Sa / G		Joel 3. 12–end Ps. 97. 1, 8–end Luke 11. 27–28	Ps. *76*; 79 1 Macc. 2. 49–end or 2 Chron. 15. 1–15 Mark 14. 66–end
15	S / G	**THE EIGHTEENTH SUNDAY AFTER TRINITY (Proper 23)** *Track 1* Exod. 32. 1–14 Ps. 106. 1–6, 19–23 (or 106. 1–6) Phil. 4. 1–9 Matt. 22. 1–14	*Track 2* Isa. 25. 1–9 Ps. 23 Phil. 4. 1–9 Matt. 22. 1–14	Ps. 138; 141 Isa. 50. 4–10 Luke 13. 22–30
16 DEL 28	M / G	*Nicholas Ridley, Bishop of London, and Hugh Latimer, Bishop of Worcester, Reformation Martyrs, 1555*	Rom. 1. 1–7 Ps. 98 Luke 11. 29–32	Ps. *80*; 82 1 Macc. 3. 1–26 or 2 Chron. 17. 1–12 Mark 15. 1–15

Second Service Evening Prayer		Calendar and Holy Communion	Morning Prayer	Evening Prayer
Ps. 38 1 Kings 18. 21–end Acts 21. 1–16	Gr	**Faith of Aquitaine, Martyr, c. 304** Com. Virgin Martyr	Wisd. 18. 6–19 or 2 Chron. 6. 22–end Mark 13. 24–31	1 Kings 18. 21–end Acts 21. 1–16
Ps. 65; **66** 1 Kings ch. 19 Acts 21. 17–36 ct	G		Wisd. ch. 19 or 2 Chron. ch. 7 Mark 13. 32–end	1 Kings ch. 19 Acts 21. 17–36 ct
		THE SEVENTEENTH SUNDAY AFTER TRINITY		
Ps. 136 (or 136. 1–9) Prov. 2. 1–11 1 John 2. 1–17 *Gospel:* Mark 10. 2–16	G	Prov. 25. 6–14 Ps. 33. 6–12 Eph. 4. 1–6 Luke 14. 1–11	Ps. 128; 129; 134 Isa. 49. 13–23 Luke 12. 1–12	Ps. 136 (or 136. 1–9) Prov. 2. 1–11 1 John 2. 1–17
Ps. **72**; 75 1 Kings ch. 21 Acts 21.37 – 22.21	Gr	**Denys, Bishop of Paris, Martyr, c. 250** Com. Martyr	1 Macc. 1. 1–19 or 2 Chron. 9. 1–12 Mark 14. 1–11	1 Kings ch. 21 Acts 21.37 – 22.21
Ps. 74 1 Kings 22. 1–28 Acts 22.22 – 23.11	G		1 Macc. 1. 20–40 or 2 Chron. 10.1 – 11.4 Mark 14. 12–25	1 Kings 22. 1–28 Acts 22.22 – 23.11
Ps. 119. 81–104 1 Kings 22. 29–45 Acts 23. 12–end	G		1 Macc. 1. 41–end or 2 Chron. ch. 12 Mark 14. 26–42	1 Kings 22. 29–45 Acts 23. 12–end
Ps. 78. 40–end† 2 Kings 1. 2–17 Acts 24. 1–23	G		1 Macc. 2. 1–28 or 2 Chron. 13.1 – 14.1 Mark 14. 43–52	2 Kings 1. 2–17 Acts 24. 1–23
Ps. 69 2 Kings 2. 1–18 Acts 24.24 – 25.12	Gw	**Edward the Confessor, King of England, 1066, translated 1163** Com. Saint	1 Macc. 2. 29–48 or 2 Chron. 14. 2–end Mark 14. 53–65	2 Kings 2. 1–18 Acts 24.24 – 25.12
Ps. 81; **84** 2 Kings 4. 1–37 Acts 25. 13–end ct	G		1 Macc. 2. 49–end or 2 Chron. 15. 1–15 Mark 14. 66–end	2 Kings 4. 1–37 Acts 25. 13–end ct
		THE EIGHTEENTH SUNDAY AFTER TRINITY		
Ps. 139. 1–18 (or 139. 1–11) Prov. 3. 1–18 1 John 3. 1–15 *Gospel:* Mark 10. 17–31	G	Deut. 6. 4–9 Ps. 122 1 Cor. 1. 4–8 Matt. 22. 34–end	Ps. 138; 141 Isa. 50. 4–10 Luke 13. 22–30	Ps. 139. 1–18 (or 139. 1–11) Prov. 3. 1–18 1 John 3. 1–15
Ps. **85**; 86 2 Kings ch. 5 Acts 26. 1–23	G		1 Macc. 3. 1–26 or 2 Chron. 17. 1–12 Mark 15. 1–15	2 Kings ch. 5 Acts 26. 1–23

October 2017

			Sunday Principal Service Weekday Eucharist		Third Service Morning Prayer
17	Tu	**Ignatius, Bishop of Antioch, Martyr, c. 107** Com. Martyr *also* Phil. 3. 7–12 John 6. 52–58	*or*	Rom. 1. 16–25 Ps. 19. 1–4 Luke 11. 37–41	Ps. 87; **89. 1–18** 1 Macc. 3. 27–41 *or* 2 Chron. 18. 1–27 Mark 15. 16–32
	Gr				
18	W	LUKE THE EVANGELIST		Isa. 35. 3–6 *or* Acts 16. 6–12a Ps. 147. 1–7 2 Tim. 4. 5–17	MP: Ps. 145; 146 Isa. ch. 55 Luke 1. 1–4
	R			Luke 10. 1–9	
19	Th	**Henry Martyn, Translator of the Scriptures, Missionary in India and Persia, 1812** Com. Missionary *esp.* Mark 16. 15–end *also* Isa. 55. 6–11	*or*	Rom. 3. 21–30 Ps. 130 Luke 11. 47–end	Ps. 90; **92** 1 Macc. 4. 1–25 *or* 2 Chron. 20. 1–23 Mark 15. 42–end
	Gw				
20	F			Rom. 4. 1–8 Ps. 32 Luke 12. 1–7	Ps. **88**; (95) 1 Macc. 4. 26–35 *or* 2 Chron. 22.10 – 23.end Mark 16. 1–8
	G				
21	Sa			Rom. 4. 13, 16–18 Ps. 105. 6–10, 41–44 Luke 12. 8–12	Ps. 96; **97**; 100 1 Macc. 4. 36–end *or* 2 Chron. 24. 1–22 Mark 16. 9–end
	G				
22	S	THE NINETEENTH SUNDAY AFTER TRINITY **(Proper 24)** *Track 1* Exod. 33. 12–end Ps. 99 1 Thess. 1. 1–10 Matt. 22. 15–22		*Track 2* Isa. 45. 1–7 Ps. 96. 1–9 [10–13] 1 Thess. 1. 1–10 Matt. 22. 15–22	Ps. 145; 149 Isa. 54. 1–14 Luke 13. 31–end
	G				
23 DEL 29	M			Rom. 4. 20–end *Canticle:* Benedictus 1–6 Luke 12. 13–21	Ps. **98**; 99; 101 1 Macc. 6. 1–17 *or* 2 Chron. 26. 1–21 John 13. 1–11
	G				
24	Tu			Rom. 5. 12, 15, 17–end Ps. 40. 7–12 Luke 12. 35–38	Ps. **106**†; (*or* 103) 1 Macc. 6. 18–47 *or* 2 Chron. ch. 28 John 13. 12–20
	G				
25	W	*Crispin and Crispinian, Martyrs at Rome, c. 287*		Rom. 6. 12–18 Ps. 124 Luke 12. 39–48	Ps. 110; **111**; 112 1 Macc. 7. 1–20 *or* 2 Chron. 29. 1–19 John 13. 21–30
	G				
26	Th	**Alfred the Great, King of the West Saxons, Scholar, 899** *Cedd, Abbot of Lastingham, Bishop of the East Saxons, 664** Com. Saint *also* 2 Sam. 23. 1–5 John 18. 33–37	*or*	Rom. 6. 19–end Ps. 1 Luke 12. 49–53	Ps. 113; **115** 1 Macc. 7. 21–end *or* 2 Chron. 29. 20–end John 13. 31–end
	Gw				
27	F			Rom. 7. 18–end Ps. 119. 33–40 Luke 12. 54–end	Ps. 139 1 Macc. 9. 1–22 *or* 2 Chron. ch. 30 John 14. 1–14
	G				

*Chad may be celebrated with Cedd on 26 October instead of 2 March.

Second Service Evening Prayer		Calendar and Holy Communion	Morning Prayer	Evening Prayer
Ps. 89. 19–end 2 Kings 6. 1–23 Acts 26. 24–end *or First EP of Luke* Ps. 33 Hos. 6. 1–3 2 Tim. 3. 10–end **R ct**	Gw	**Etheldreda, Abbess of Ely, 679** Com. Abbess	1 Macc. 3. 27–41 *or 2 Chron. 18. 1–27* Mark 15. 16–32	2 Kings 6. 1–23 Acts 26. 24–end *or First EP of Luke* (Ps. 33) Hos. 6. 1–3 2 Tim. 3. 10–end **R ct**
EP: Ps. 103 Ecclus. 38. 1–14 *or Isa. 61. 1–6* Col. 4. 7–end	R	**LUKE THE EVANGELIST** Isa. 35. 3–6 Ps. 147. 1–6 2 Tim. 4. 5–15 Luke 10. 1–9 *or Luke 7. 36–end*	(Ps. 145; 146) Isa. ch. 55 Luke 1. 1–4	(Ps. 103) Ecclus. 38. 1–14 *or Isa. 61. 1–6* Col. 4. 7–end
Ps. 94 2 Kings 9. 17–end Acts 27. 27–end	G		1 Macc. 4. 1–25 *or 2 Chron. 20. 1–23* Mark 15. 42–end	2 Kings 9. 17–end Acts 27. 27–end
Ps. 102 2 Kings 12. 1–19 Acts 28. 1–16	G		1 Macc. 4. 26–35 *or 2 Chron. 22.10 – 23.end* Mark 16. 1–8	2 Kings 12. 1–19 Acts 28. 1–16
Ps. 104 2 Kings 17. 1–23 Acts 28. 17–end **ct**	G		1 Macc. 4. 36–end *or 2 Chron. 24. 1–22* Mark 16. 9–end	2 Kings 17. 1–23 Acts 28. 17–end **ct**
Ps. 142 [143. 1–11] Prov. 4. 1–18 1 John 3.16 – 4.6 *Gospel*: Mark 10. 35–45	G	**THE NINETEENTH SUNDAY AFTER TRINITY** Gen. 18. 23–32 Ps. 141. 1–9 Eph. 4. 17–end Matt. 9. 1–8	Ps. 138 Isa. 54. 1–14 Luke 13. 31–end	Ps. 142 [143. 1–11] Prov. 4. 1–18 1 John 3.16 – 4.6
Ps. *105*† (or 103) 2 Kings 17. 24–end Phil. 1. 1–11	G		1 Macc. 6. 1–17 *or 2 Chron. 26. 1–21* John 13. 1–11	2 Kings 17. 24–end Phil. 1. 1–11
Ps. 107† 2 Kings 18. 1–12 Phil. 1. 12–end	G		1 Macc. 6. 18–47 *or 2 Chron. ch. 28* John 13. 12–20	2 Kings 18. 1–12 Phil. 1. 12–end
Ps. 119. 129–152 2 Kings 18. 13–end Phil. 2. 1–13	Gr	**Crispin, Martyr at Rome, c. 287** Com. Martyr	1 Macc. 7. 1–20 *or 2 Chron. 29. 1–19* John 13. 21–30	2 Kings 18. 13–end Phil. 2. 1–13
Ps. 114; *116*; 117 2 Kings 19. 1–19 Phil. 2. 14–end	G		1 Macc. 7. 21–end *or 2 Chron. 29. 20–end* John 13. 31–end	2 Kings 19. 1–19 Phil. 2. 14–end
Ps. *130*; 131; 137 2 Kings 19. 20–36 Phil. 3.1 – 4.1 *or First EP of Simon and Jude* Ps. 124; 125; 126 Deut. 32. 1–4 John 14. 15–26 **R ct**	G		1 Macc. 9. 1–22 *or 2 Chron. ch. 30* John 14. 1–14	2 Kings 19. 20–36 Phil. 3.1 – 4.1 *or First EP of Simon and Jude* (Ps. 124; 125; 126) Deut. 32. 1–4 John 14. 15–26 **R ct**

October 2017

			Sunday Principal Service / Weekday Eucharist	Third Service / Morning Prayer

28 Sa — SIMON AND JUDE, APOSTLES

R

Isa. 28. 14–16
Ps. 119. 89–96
Eph. 2. 19–end
John 15. 17–end

MP: Ps. 116; 117
Wisd. 5. 1–16
or Isa. 45. 18–end
Luke 6. 12–16

29 S — THE LAST SUNDAY AFTER TRINITY **(Proper 25)***

Track 1
Deut. 34. 1–12
Ps. 90. 1–6, 13–17 (or 90. 1–6)
1 Thess. 2. 1–8
Matt. 22. 34–end

G

Track 2
Lev. 19. 1–2, 15–18
Ps. 1
1 Thess. 2. 1–8
Matt. 22. 34–end

Ps. 119. 137–152
Isa. 59. 9–20
Luke 14. 1–14

or, if being observed as Bible Sunday:

Neh. 8. 1–4a [5–6] 8–12
Ps. 119. 9–16
Col. 3. 12–17
Matt. 24. 30–35

G

Ps. 119. 137–152
Deut. 17. 14–15, 18–end
John 5. 36b–end

30 M
DEL 30

G

Rom. 8. 12–17
Ps. 68. 1–6, 19
Luke 13. 10–17

Ps. 123; 124; 125; *126*
2 Macc. 4. 7–17
or 2 Chron. 33. 1–13
John 15. 1–11

31 Tu — *Martin Luther, Reformer, 1546*

Rom. 8. 18–25
Ps. 126
Luke 13. 18–21

Ps. *132*; 133
2 Macc. 6. 12–end
or 2 Chron. 34. 1–18
John 15. 12–17

G

November 2017

1 W — **ALL SAINTS' DAY**

𝇇

Rev. 7. 9–end
Ps. 34. 1–10
1 John 3. 1–3
Matt. 5. 1–12

MP: Ps. 15; 84; 149
Isa. ch. 35
Luke 9. 18–27

or, if the readings above are used on Sunday 5 November:

𝇇

Isa. 56. 3–8
or 2 Esdras 2. 42–end
Ps. 33. 1–5
Heb. 12. 18–24
Matt. 5. 1–12

MP: Ps. 111; 112; 117
Wisd. 5. 1–16
or Jer. 31. 31–34
2 Cor. 4. 5–12

or, if kept as a feria:

G

Rom. 8. 26–30
Ps. 13
Luke 13. 22–30

Ps. 119. 153–end
2 Macc. 7. 1–19
or 2 Chron. 34. 19–end
John 15. 18–end

2 Th — **Commemoration of the Faithful Departed (All Souls' Day)**

Lam. 3. 17–26, 31–33
or Wisd. 3. 1–9
Ps. 23
or Ps. 27. 1–6, 16–end
Rom. 5. 5–11
or 1 Pet. 1. 3–9
John 5. 19–25
or John 6. 37–40

Rp or Gp

or Rom. 8. 31–end
Ps. 109. 20–26, 29–30
Luke 13. 31–end

Ps. *143*; 146
2 Macc. 7. 20–41
or 2 Chron. 35. 1–19
John 16. 1–15

3 F — **Richard Hooker, Priest, Anglican Apologist, Teacher, 1600**
Martin of Porres, Friar, 1639

Com. Teacher
esp. John 16. 12–15
also Ecclus. 44. 10–15

Rw or Gw

or Rom. 9. 1–5
Ps. 147. 13–end
Luke 14. 1–6

Ps. 142; *144*
Tobit ch. 1
or 2 Chron. 35.20 – 36.10
John 16. 16–22

*If the Dedication Festival is kept on this Sunday, use the provision given on 30 September and 1 October.

Second Service Evening Prayer	Calendar and Holy Communion		Morning Prayer	Evening Prayer
EP: Ps. 119. 1–16 1 Macc. 2. 42–66 *or* Jer. 3. 11–18 Jude 1–4, 17–end	**SIMON AND JUDE, APOSTLES** Isa. 28. 9–16 Ps. 116. 11–end Jude 1–8 *or* Rev. 21. 9–14 John 15. 17–end	R	(Ps. 119. 89–96) Wisd. 5. 1–16 *or* Isa. 45. 18–end Luke 6. 12–16	(Ps. 119. 1–16) 1 Macc. 2. 42–66 *or* Jer. 3. 11–18 Eph. 2. 19–end
Ps. 119. 89–104 Eccles. chs 11 and 12 2 Tim. 2. 1–7 *Gospel:* Mark 12. 28–34 Ps. 119. 89–104 Isa. 55. 1–11 Luke 4. 14–30	**THE TWENTIETH SUNDAY AFTER TRINITY** Prov. 9. 1–6 Ps. 145. 15–end Eph. 5. 15–21 Matt. 22. 1–14	G	Ps. 119. 137–152 Isa. 59. 9–20 Luke 14. 11–24	Ps. 119. 89–104 Eccles. chs 11 and 12 2 Tim. 2. 1–7
Ps. *127*; 128; 129 2 Kings 21. 1–18 1 Tim. 1. 1–17		G	2 Macc. 4. 7–17 *or* 2 Chron. 33. 1–13 John 15. 1–11	2 Kings 21. 1–18 1 Tim. 1. 1–17
First EP of All Saints Ps. 1; 5 Ecclus. 44. 1–15 *or* Isa. 40. 27–end Rev. 19. 6–10 𝔚 ct *or, if All Saints is observed on* *5 November* Ps. (134); *135* 2 Kings 22.1 – 23.3 1 Tim. 1.18 – 2.end		G	2 Macc. 6. 12–end *or* 2 Chron. 34. 1–18 John 15. 12–17	*First EP of All Saints* Ps. 1; 5 Ecclus. 44. 1–15 *or* Isa. 40. 27–end Rev. 19. 6–10 𝔚 ct
EP: Ps. 148; 150 Isa. 65. 17–end Heb. 11.32 – 12.2 *EP*: Ps. 145 Isa. 66. 20–23 Col. 1. 9–14 Ps. 136 2 Kings 23. 4–25 1 Tim. ch. 3	**ALL SAINTS' DAY** Isa. 66. 20–23 Ps. 33. 1–5 Rev. 7. 2–4 [5–8] 9–12 Matt. 5. 1–12	𝔚	Ps. 15; 84; 149 Isa. ch. 35 Luke 9. 18–27	Ps. 148; 150 Isa. 65. 17–end Heb. 11.32 – 12.2
Ps. *138*; 140; 141 2 Kings. 23.36 – 24.17 1 Tim. ch. 4	To celebrate All Souls' Day, see *Common Worship* provision.	G	2 Macc. 7. 20–41 *or* 2 Chron. 35. 1–19 John 16. 1–15	2 Kings. 23.36 – 24.17 1 Tim. ch. 4
Ps. 145 2 Kings 24.18 – 25.12 1 Tim. 5. 1–16		G	Tobit ch. 1 *or* 2 Chron. 35.20 – 36.10 John 16. 16–22	2 Kings 24.18 – 25.12 1 Tim. 5. 1–16

November 2017

			Sunday Principal Service Weekday Eucharist	Third Service Morning Prayer
4	Sa R *or* G		Rom. 11. 1–2, 11–12, 25–29 Ps. 94. 14–19 Luke 14. 1, 7–11	Ps. 147 Tobit ch. 2 *or* 2 Chron. 36. 11–end John 16. 23–end
5	S R *or* G ℣	**THE FOURTH SUNDAY BEFORE ADVENT** *Or ALL SAINTS' SUNDAY (see readings for 1 November throughout the day)*	Micah 3. 5–end Ps. 43 *or* Ps. 107. 1–8 1 Thess. 2. 9–13 Matt. 24. 1–14	Ps. 33 Isa. 66. 20–23 Eph. 1. 11–end
6 DEL 31	M R *or* G	*Leonard, Hermit, 6th century; William Temple, Archbishop of Canterbury, Teacher, 1944*	Rom. 11. 29–end Ps. 69. 31–37 Luke 14. 12–14	Ps. 2; 146 *alt.* Ps. 1; 2; 3 Isa. 1. 1–20 Matt. 1. 18–end
7	Tu Rw *or* Gw	**Willibrord of York, Bishop, Apostle of Frisia, 739** Com. Missionary *or* *esp.* Isa. 52. 7–10 Matt. 28. 16–end	Rom. 12. 5–16 Ps. 131 Luke 14. 15–24	Ps. 5; 147. 1–12 *alt.* Ps. 5; 6; (8) Isa. 1. 21–end Matt. 2. 1–15
8	W Rw *or* Gw	**The Saints and Martyrs of England** Isa. 61. 4–9 *or* Ecclus. 44. 1–15 Ps. 15 Rev. 19. 5–10 John 17. 18–23	Rom. 13. 8–10 Ps. 112 Luke 14. 25–33	Ps. 9; 147. 13–end *alt.* Ps. 119. 1–32 Isa. 2. 1–11 Matt. 2. 16–end
9	Th R *or* G	*Margery Kempe, Mystic, c. 1440*	Rom. 14. 7–12 Ps. 27. 14–end Luke 15. 1–10	Ps. 11; 15; 148 *alt.* Ps. 14; 15; 16 Isa. 2. 12–end Matt. ch. 3
10	F Rw *or* Gw	**Leo the Great, Bishop of Rome, Teacher, 461** Com. Teacher *or* *also* 1 Pet. 5. 1–11	Rom. 15. 14–21 Ps. 98 Luke 16. 1–8	Ps. 16; 149 *alt.* Ps. 17; 19 Isa. 3. 1–15 Matt. 4. 1–11
11	Sa Rw *or* Gw	**Martin, Bishop of Tours, c. 397** Com. Bishop *or* *also* 1 Thess. 5. 1–11 Matt. 25. 34–40	Rom. 16. 3–9, 16, 22–end Ps. 145. 1–7 Luke 16. 9–15	Ps. 18. 31–end; 150 *alt.* Ps. 20; 21; 23 Isa. 4.2 – 5.7 Matt. 4. 12–22
12	S R *or* G	**THE THIRD SUNDAY BEFORE ADVENT** (Remembrance Sunday) Wisd. 6. 12–16 *or* *Canticle:* Wisd. 6. 17–20 1 Thess. 4. 13–end Matt. 25. 1–13	Amos 5. 18–24 Ps. 70 1 Thess. 4. 13–end Matt. 25. 1–13	Ps. 91 Deut. 17. 14–end 1 Tim. 2. 1–7
13 DEL 32	M Rw *or* Gw	**Charles Simeon, Priest, Evangelical Divine, 1836** Com. Pastor *or* *esp.* Mal. 2. 5–7 *also* Col. 1. 3–8 Luke 8. 4–8	Wisd. 1. 1–7 *or* Titus 1. 1–9 Ps. 139. 1–9 *or* Ps. 24. 1–6 Luke 17. 1–6	Ps. 19; 20 *alt.* Ps. 27; 30 Isa. 5. 8–24 Matt. 4.23 – 5.12
14	Tu R *or* G	*Samuel Seabury, first Anglican Bishop in North America, 1796*	Wisd. 2.23 – 3.9 *or* Titus 2. 1–8, 11–14 Ps. 34. 1–6 *or* Ps. 37. 3–5, 30–32 Luke 17. 7–10	Ps. 21; 24 *alt.* Ps. 32; 36 Isa. 5. 25–end Matt. 5. 13–20

Second Service Evening Prayer	Calendar and Holy Communion	Morning Prayer	Evening Prayer
Ps. *148*; 149; 150 2 Kings 25. 22–end 1 Tim. 5. 17–end ct	G	Tobit ch. 2 *or* 2 Chron. 36. 11–end John 16. 23–end	2 Kings 25. 22–end 1 Tim. 5. 17–end ct
	THE TWENTY-FIRST SUNDAY AFTER TRINITY		
Ps. 111; 117 Dan. 7. 1–18 Luke 6. 17–31	Gen. 32. 24–29 Ps. 90. 1–12 Eph. 6. 10–20 John 4. 46b–end G	Ps. 33 Isa. 66. 20–23 Eph. 1. 11–end	Ps. 111; 117 Dan. 7. 1–18 Luke 6. 17–31
Ps. *92*; 96; 97 *alt.* Ps. *4*; 7 Dan. ch. 1 Rev. ch. 1	**Leonard, Hermit, 6th century** Com. Abbot Gw	Isa. 1. 1–20 Matt. 1. 18–end	Dan. ch. 1 Rev. ch. 1
Ps. 98; 99; *100* *alt.* Ps. *9*; 10† Dan. 2. 1–24 Rev. 2. 1–11	G	Isa. 1. 21–end Matt. 2. 1–15	Dan. 2. 1–24 Rev. 2. 1–11
Ps. 111; *112*; 116 *alt.* Ps. *11*; 12; 13 Dan. 2. 25–end Rev. 2. 12–end	G	Isa. 2. 1–11 Matt. 2. 16–end	Dan. 2. 25–end Rev. 2. 12–end
Ps. 118 *alt.* Ps. 18† Dan. 3. 1–18 Rev. 3. 1–13	G	Isa. 2. 12–end Matt. ch. 3	Dan. 3. 1–18 Rev. 3. 1–13
Ps. 137; 138; *143* *alt.* Ps. 22 Dan. 3. 19–end Rev. 3. 14–end	G	Isa. 3. 1–15 Matt. 4. 1–11	Dan. 3. 19–end Rev. 3. 14–end
Ps. 145 *alt.* Ps. *24*; 25 Dan. 4. 1–18 Rev. ch. 4 ct	**Martin, Bishop of Tours, c. 397** Com. Bishop Gw	Isa. 4.2 – 5.7 Matt. 4. 12–22	Dan. 4. 1–18 Rev. ch. 4 ct
	THE TWENTY-SECOND SUNDAY AFTER TRINITY		
Ps. [20]; 82 Judg. 7. 2–22 John 15. 9–17	Gen. 45. 1–7, 15 Ps. 133 Phil. 1. 3–11 Matt. 18. 21–end G	Ps. 91 Deut. 17. 14–end 1 Tim. 2. 1–7	Ps. [20]; 82 Judg. 7. 2–22 John 15. 9–17
Ps. 34 *alt.* Ps. 26; *28*; 29 Dan. 4. 19–end Rev. ch. 5	**Britius, Bishop of Tours, 444** Com. Bishop Gw	Isa. 5. 8–24 Matt. 4.23 – 5.12	Dan. 4. 19–end Rev. ch. 5
Ps. 36; *40* *alt.* Ps. 33 Dan. 5. 1–12 Rev. ch. 6	G	Isa. 5. 25–end Matt. 5. 13–20	Dan. 5. 1–12 Rev. ch. 6

November 2017

		Sunday Principal Service / Weekday Eucharist	Third Service / Morning Prayer

15 W

	Sunday Principal Service / Weekday Eucharist	Third Service / Morning Prayer
	Wisd. 6. 1–11	Ps. **23**; 25
	or Titus 3. 1–7	alt. Ps. 34
	Ps. 82	Isa. ch. 6
	or Ps. 23	Matt. 5. 21–37
R or G	Luke 17. 11–19	

16 Th

Margaret, Queen of Scotland, Philanthropist, Reformer of the Church, 1093
Edmund Rich of Abingdon, Archbishop of Canterbury, 1240

Com. Saint	*or*	Wisd. 7.22 – 8.1	Ps. **26**; 27
also Prov. 31. 10–12, 20, 26–end		or Philemon 7–20	alt. Ps. 37†
1 Cor. 12.13 – 13.3		Ps. 119. 89–96	Isa. 7. 1–17
Matt. 25. 34–end		or Ps. 146. 4–end	Matt. 5. 38–end
Rw or Gw		Luke 17. 20–25	

17 F

Hugh, Bishop of Lincoln, 1200

Com. Bishop	*or*	Wisd. 13. 1–9	Ps. 28; **32**
also 1 Tim. 6. 11–16		or 2 John 4–9	alt. Ps. 31
		Ps. 19. 1–4	Isa. 8. 1–15
		or Ps. 119. 1–8	Matt. 6. 1–18
Rw or Gw		Luke 17. 26–end	

18 Sa

Elizabeth of Hungary, Princess of Thuringia, Philanthropist, 1231

Com. Saint	*or*	Wisd. 18. 14–16; 19. 6–9	Ps. 33
esp. Matt. 25. 31–end		or 3 John 5–8	alt. Ps. 41; **42**; 43
also Prov. 31. 10–end		Ps. 105. 1–5, 35–42	Isa. 8.16 – 9.7
		or Ps. 112	Matt. 6. 19–end
Rw or Gw		Luke 18. 1–8	

19 S

THE SECOND SUNDAY BEFORE ADVENT

	Zeph. 1. 7, 12–end	Ps. 98
	Ps. 90. 1–8 [9–11] 12	Dan. 10. 19–end
	(or 90. 1–8)	Rev. ch. 4
	1 Thess. 5. 1–11	
R or G	Matt. 25. 14–30	

20 M
DEL 33

Edmund, King of the East Angles, Martyr, 870
Priscilla Lydia Sellon, a Restorer of the Religious Life in the Church of England, 1876

Com. Martyr	*or*	1 Macc. 1. 10–15,	Ps. 46; **47**
also Prov. 20. 28; 21. 1–4, 7		41–43, 54–57, 62–64	alt. Ps. 44
		or Rev. 1. 1–4; 2. 1–5	Isa. 9.8 – 10.4
		Ps. 79. 1–5	Matt. 7. 1–12
		or Ps. 1	
R or Gr		Luke 18. 35–end	

21 Tu

	Sunday Principal Service / Weekday Eucharist	Third Service / Morning Prayer
	2 Macc. 6. 18–end	Ps. 48; **52**
	or Rev. 3. 1–6, 14–31	alt. Ps. **48**; 52
	Ps. 11	Isa. 10. 5–19
	or Ps. 15	Matt. 7. 13–end
R or G	Luke 19. 1–10	

22 W

Cecilia, Martyr at Rome, c. 230

	Sunday Principal Service / Weekday Eucharist	Third Service / Morning Prayer
	2 Macc. 7. 1, 20–31	Ps. **56**; 57
	or Rev. ch. 4	alt. Ps. 119. 57–80
	Ps. 116. 10–end	Isa. 10. 20–32
	or Ps. 150	Matt. 8. 1–13
R or G	Luke 19. 11–28	

23 Th

Clement, Bishop of Rome, Martyr, c. 100

Com. Martyr	*or*	1 Macc. 2. 15–29	Ps. 61; **62**
also Phil. 3.17 – 4.3		or Rev. 5. 1–10	alt. Ps. 56; **57**; (63†)
Matt. 16. 13–19		Ps. 129	Isa. 10.33 – 11.9
		or Ps. 149. 1–5	Matt. 8. 14–22
R or Gr		Luke 19. 41–44	

24 F

	Sunday Principal Service / Weekday Eucharist	Third Service / Morning Prayer
	1 Macc. 4. 36–37, 52–59	Ps. **63**; 65
	or Rev. 10. 8–11	alt. Ps. **51**; 54
	Ps. 122	Isa. 11.10 – 12.end
	or Ps. 119. 65–72	Matt. 8. 23–end
R or G	Luke 19. 45–48	

Second Service Evening Prayer		Calendar and Holy Communion	Morning Prayer	Evening Prayer
Ps. 37 *alt.* Ps. 119. 33–56 Dan. 5. 13–end Rev. 7. 1–4, 9–end	Gw	**Machutus, Bishop, Apostle of Brittany, c. 564** Com. Bishop	Isa. ch. 6 Matt. 5. 21–37	Dan. 5. 13–end Rev. 7. 1–4, 9–end
Ps. 42; *43* *alt.* Ps. 39; *40* Dan. ch. 6 Rev. ch. 8	G		Isa. 7. 1–17 Matt. 5. 38–end	Dan. ch. 6 Rev. ch. 8
Ps. 31 *alt.* Ps. 35 Dan. 7. 1–14 Rev. 9. 1–12	Gw	**Hugh, Bishop of Lincoln, 1200** Com. Bishop	Isa. 8. 1–15 Matt. 6. 1–18	Dan. 7. 1–14 Rev. 9. 1–12
Ps. 84; *86* *alt.* Ps. 45; *46* Dan. 7. 15–end Rev. 9. 13–end ct	G		Isa. 8.16 – 9.7 Matt. 6. 19–end	Dan. 7. 15–end Rev. 9. 13–end ct
Ps. 89. 19–37 (or 89. 19–29) 1 Kings 1. [1–14] 15–40 Rev. 1. 4–18 *Gospel:* Luke 9. 1–6	G	THE TWENTY-THIRD SUNDAY AFTER TRINITY Isa. 11. 1–10 Ps. 44. 1–9 Phil. 3. 17–end Matt. 22. 15–22	Ps. 98 Dan. 10. 19–end Rev. ch. 4	Ps. 89. 19–37 (or 89. 19–29) 1 Kings 1. [1–14] 15–40 Rev. 1. 4–18
Ps. 70; *71* *alt.* Ps. *47*; 49 Dan. 8. 1–14 Rev. ch. 10	Gr	**Edmund, King of the East Angles, Martyr, 870** Com. Martyr	Isa. 9.8 – 10.4 Matt. 7. 1–12	Dan. 8. 1–14 Rev. ch. 10
Ps. *67*; 72 *alt.* Ps. 50 Dan. 8. 15–end Rev. 11. 1–14	G		Isa. 10. 5–19 Matt. 7. 13–end	Dan. 8. 15–end Rev. 11. 1–14
Ps. 73 *alt.* Ps. *59*; 60; (67) Dan. 9. 1–19 Rev. 11. 15–end	Gr	**Cecilia, Martyr at Rome, c. 230** Com. Virgin Martyr	Isa. 10. 20–32 Matt. 8. 1–13	Dan. 9. 1–19 Rev. 11. 15–end
Ps. 74; *76* *alt.* Ps. 61; *62*; 64 Dan. 9. 20–end Rev. ch. 12	Gr	**Clement, Bishop of Rome, Martyr, c. 100** Com. Martyr	Isa. 10.33 – 11.9 Matt. 8. 14–22	Dan. 9. 20–end Rev. ch. 12
Ps. 77 *alt.* Ps. 38 Dan. 10.1 – 11.1 Rev. 13. 1–10	G		Isa. 11.10 – 12.end Matt. 8. 23–end	Dan. 10.1 – 11.1 Rev. 13. 1–10

November 2017

		Sunday Principal Service / Weekday Eucharist	Third Service / Morning Prayer
25	Sa	*Catherine of Alexandria, Martyr, 4th century; Isaac Watts, Hymn Writer, 1748*	
		1 Macc. 6. 1–13	Ps. 78. 1–39
		or Rev. 11. 4–12	*alt.* Ps. 68
		Ps. 124	Isa. 13. 1–13
		or Ps. 144. 1–9	Matt. 9. 1–17
		Luke 20. 27–40	
	R *or* G		
26	S	**CHRIST THE KING**	
		The Sunday Next Before Advent	
		Ezek. 34. 11–16, 20–24	MP: Ps. 29; 110
		Ps. 95. 1–7	Isa. 4.2 – 5.7
	R *or* W	Eph. 1. 15–end	Luke 19. 29–38
		Matt. 25. 31–end	
27 DEL 34	M	Dan. 1. 1–6, 8–20	Ps. 92; **96**
		Canticle: Bless the Lord	*alt.* Ps. 71
		Luke 21. 1–4	Isa. 14. 3–20
	R *or* G		Matt. 9. 18–34
28	Tu	Dan. 2. 31–45	Ps. **97**; 98; 100
		Canticle: Benedicite 1–3	*alt.* Ps. 73
		Luke 21. 5–11	Isa. ch. 17
	R *or* G		Matt. 9.35 – 10.15
29	W	Dan. 5. 1–6, 13–14, 16–17, 23–28	Ps. 110; 111; *112*
			alt. Ps. 77
		Canticle: Benedicite 4–5	Isa. ch. 19
		Luke 21. 12–19	Matt. 10. 16–33
	R *or* G		
		Day of Intercession and Thanksgiving for the Missionary Work of the Church	
		Isa. 49. 1–6; Isa. 52. 7–10; Mic. 4. 1–5	
		Acts 17. 12–end; 2 Cor. 5.14 – 6.2; Eph. 2. 13–end	
		Ps. 2; 46; 47	
		Matt. 5. 13–16; Matt. 28. 16–end; John 17. 20–end	
30	Th	**ANDREW THE APOSTLE**	
		Isa. 52. 7–10	MP: Ps. 47; 147. 1–12
		Ps. 19. 1–6	Ezek. 47. 1–12
	R	Rom. 10. 12–18	*or* Ecclus. 14. 20–end
		Matt. 4. 18–22	John 12. 20–32

December 2017

		Sunday Principal Service / Weekday Eucharist	Third Service / Morning Prayer
1	F	*Charles de Foucauld, Hermit in the Sahara, 1916*	
		Dan. 7. 2–14	Ps. 139
		Canticle: Benedicite 8b–10a	*alt.* Ps. 55
	R *or* G	Luke 21. 29–33	Isa. 22. 1–14
			Matt. 11. 2–19
2	Sa	Dan. 7. 15–27	Ps. 145
		Canticle: Benedicite 10b–end	*alt.* Ps. **76**; 79
		Luke 21. 34–36	Isa. ch. 24
	R *or* G		Matt. 11. 20–end

Second Service Evening Prayer		Calendar and Holy Communion	Morning Prayer	Evening Prayer
		Catherine of Alexandria, Martyr, 4th century		
Ps. 78. 40—end		Com. Virgin Martyr	Isa. 13. 1–13	Dan. ch. 12
alt. Ps. 65; *66*			Matt. 9. 1–17	Rev. 13. 11—end
Dan. ch. 12				
Rev. 13. 11—end				
ct				
or First EP of Christ the King				
Ps. 99; 100				
Isa. 10.33 – 11.9				
1 Tim. 6. 11–16				
R *or* **W ct**	Gr			ct
		THE SUNDAY NEXT BEFORE ADVENT		
		To celebrate Christ the King, see *Common Worship* provision.		
EP: Ps. 93; [97]		Jer. 23. 5–8	Ps. 29; 110	Ps. 93; [97]
2 Sam. 23. 1–7		Ps. 85. 8—end	Isa. 4.2 – 5.7	2 Sam. 23. 1–7
or 1 Macc. 2. 15–29		Col. 1. 13–20	Luke 19. 29–38	*or* 1 Macc. 2. 15–29
Matt. 28. 16—end	G	John 6. 5–14		Matt. 28. 16—end
Ps. *80*; 81			Isa. 14. 3–20	Isa. 40. 1–11
alt. Ps. *72*; 75			Matt. 9. 18–34	Rev. 14. 1–13
Isa. 40. 1–11				
Rev. 14. 1–13	G			
Ps. 99; *101*			Isa. ch. 17	Isa. 40. 12–26
alt. Ps. 74			Matt. 9.35 – 10.15	Rev. 14.14 – 15.end
Isa. 40. 12–26				
Rev. 14.14 – 15.end	G			
Ps. 121; *122*; 123; 124			Isa. ch. 19	Isa. 40.27 – 41.7
alt. Ps. 119. 81–104			Matt. 10. 16–33	Rev. 16. 1–11
Isa. 40.27 – 41.7				*or First EP of*
Rev. 16. 1–11				*Andrew the Apostle*
or First EP of Andrew				(Ps. 48)
the Apostle				Isa. 49. 1–9a
Ps. 48				1 Cor. 4. 9–16
Isa. 49. 1–9a				
1 Cor. 4. 9–16				
R ct	G			**R ct**
		To celebrate the Day of Intercession and Thanksgiving for the Missionary Work of the Church, see *Common Worship* provision.		
		ANDREW THE APOSTLE		
EP: Ps. 87; 96		Zech. 8. 20—end	(Ps. 47; 147. 1–12)	(Ps. 87; 96)
Zech. 8. 20—end		Ps. 92. 1–5	Ezek. 47. 1–12	Isa. 52. 7–10
John 1. 35–42		Rom. 10. 9—end	*or* Ecclus. 14. 20—end	John 1. 35–42
	R	Matt. 4. 18–22	John 12. 20–32	
Ps. *146*; 147			Isa. 22. 1–14	Isa. 41.21 – 42.9
alt. Ps. 69			Matt. 11. 2–19	Rev. ch. 17
Isa. 41.21 – 42.9				
Rev. ch. 17	G			
Ps. 148; 149; *150*			Isa. ch. 24	Isa. 42. 10–17
alt. Ps. 81; *84*			Matt. 11. 20—end	Rev. ch. 18
Isa. 42. 10–17				
Rev. ch. 18				
P ct	G			**P ct**

December 2017

			Sunday Principal Service Weekday Eucharist	Third Service Morning Prayer
3	S P	**THE FIRST SUNDAY OF ADVENT** CW Year B begins	Isa. 64. 1–9 Ps. 80. 1–8, 18–20 (or 80. 1–8) 1 Cor. 1. 3–9 Mark 13. 24–end	Ps. 44 Isa. 2. 1–5 Luke 12. 35–48
4	M P	*John of Damascus, Monk, Teacher, c. 749; Nicholas Ferrar, Deacon, Founder of the Little Gidding Community, 1637* Daily Eucharistic Lectionary Year 2 begins	Isa. 2. 1–5 Ps. 122 Matt. 8. 5–11	Ps. **50**; 54 *alt.* Ps. **1**; 2; 3 Isa. 25. 1–9 Matt. 12. 1–21
5	Tu P		Isa. 11. 1–10 Ps. 72. 1–4, 18–19 Luke 10. 21–24	Ps. **80**; 82 *alt.* Ps. **5**; 6; (8) Isa. 26. 1–13 Matt. 12. 22–37
6	W Pw	**Nicholas, Bishop of Myra, c. 326** Com. Bishop *or* *also* Isa. 61. 1–3 1 Tim. 6. 6–11 Mark 10. 13–16	Isa. 25. 6–10a Ps. 23 Matt. 15. 29–37	Ps. 5; **7** *alt.* Ps. 119. 1–32 Isa. 28. 1–13 Matt. 12. 38–end
7	Th Pw	**Ambrose, Bishop of Milan, Teacher, 397** Com. Teacher *or* *also* Isa. 41. 9b–13 Luke 22. 24–30	Isa. 26. 1–6 Ps. 118. 18–27a Matt. 7. 21, 24–27	Ps. **42**; 43 *alt.* Ps. 14; **15**; 16 Isa. 28. 14–end Matt. 13. 1–23
8	F Pw	**The Conception of the Blessed Virgin Mary** Com. BVM *or*	Isa. 29. 17–end Ps. 27. 1–4, 16–17 Matt. 9. 27–31	Ps. **25**; 26 *alt.* Ps. 17; **19** Isa. 29. 1–14 Matt. 13. 24–43
9	Sa P		Isa. 30. 19–21, 23–26 Ps. 146. 4–9 Matt. 9.35 – 10.1, 6–8	Ps. **9**; (10) *alt.* Ps. 20; 21; **23** Isa. 29. 15–end Matt. 13. 44–end
10	S P	**THE SECOND SUNDAY OF ADVENT**	Isa. 40. 1–11 Ps. 85. 1–2, 8–end (or 85. 8–end) 2 Pet. 3. 8–15a Mark 1. 1–8	Ps. 80 Baruch 5. 1–9 *or* Zeph. 3. 14–end Luke 1. 5–20
11	M P		Isa. ch. 35 Ps. 85. 7–end Luke 5. 17–26	Ps. 44 *alt.* Ps. 27; **30** Isa. 30. 1–18 Matt. 14. 1–12
12	Tu P		Isa. 40. 1–11 Ps. 96. 1, 10–end Matt. 18. 12–14	Ps. **56**; 57 *alt.* Ps. 32; **36** Isa. 30. 19–end Matt. 14. 13–end
13	W Pr	**Lucy, Martyr at Syracuse, 304** Ember Day* *Samuel Johnson, Moralist, 1784* Com. Martyr *or* *also* Wisd. 3. 1–7 2 Cor. 4. 6–15	Isa. 40. 25–end Ps. 103. 8–13 Matt. 11. 28–end	Ps. **62**; 63 *alt.* Ps. 34 Isa. ch. 31 Matt. 15. 1–20
14	Th Pw	**John of the Cross, Poet, Teacher, 1591** Com. Teacher *or* *esp.* 1 Cor. 2. 1–10 *also* John 14. 18–23	Isa. 41. 13–20 Ps. 145. 1, 8–13 Matt. 11. 11–15	Ps. 53; **54**; 60 *alt.* Ps. 37† Isa. ch. 32 Matt. 15. 21–28

*For Ember Day provision, see p. 11.

Second Service Evening Prayer		Calendar and Holy Communion	Morning Prayer	Evening Prayer
Ps. 25 (or 25. 1–9) Isa. 1. 1–20 Matt. 21. 1–13	P	**THE FIRST SUNDAY IN ADVENT** Advent 1 Collect until Christmas Eve Mic. 4. 1–4, 6–7 Ps. 25. 1–9 Rom. 13. 8–14 Matt. 21. 1–13	Ps. 44 Isa. 2. 1–5 Luke 12. 35–48	Ps. 9 Isa. 1. 1–20 Mark 13. 24–end
Ps. 70; *71* alt. Ps. **4**; 7 Isa. 42. 18–end Rev. ch. 19	P		Isa. 25. 1–9 Matt. 12. 1–21	Isa. 42. 18–end Rev. ch. 19
Ps. **74**; 75 alt. Ps. **9**; 10† Isa. 43. 1–13 Rev. ch. 20	P		Isa. 26. 1–13 Matt. 12. 22–37	Isa. 43. 1–13 Rev. ch. 20
Ps. 76; **77** alt. Ps. **11**; 12; 13 Isa. 43. 14–end Rev. 21. 1–8	Pw	**Nicholas, Bishop of Myra, c. 326** Com. Bishop	Isa. 28. 1–13 Matt. 12. 38–end	Isa. 43. 14–end Rev. 21. 1–8
Ps. **40**; 46 alt. Ps. 18† Isa. 44. 1–8 Rev. 21. 9–21	P		Isa. 28. 14–end Matt. 13. 1–23	Isa. 44. 1–8 Rev. 21. 9–21
Ps. 16; *17* alt. Ps. 22 Isa. 44. 9–23 Rev. 21.22 – 22.5	Pw	**The Conception of the Blessed Virgin Mary**	Isa. 29. 1–14 Matt. 13. 24–43	Isa. 44. 9–23 Rev. 21.22 – 22.5
Ps. *27*; 28 alt. Ps. **24**; 25 Isa. 44.24 – 45.13 Rev. 22. 6–end ct	P		Isa. 29. 15–end Matt. 13. 44–end	Isa. 44.24 – 45.13 Rev. 22. 6–end ct
Ps. 40 (or 40. 12–end) 1 Kings 22. 1–28 Rom. 15. 4–13 *Gospel:* Matt. 11. 2–11	P	**THE SECOND SUNDAY IN ADVENT** 2 Kings 22. 8–10; 23. 1–3 Ps. 50. 1–6 Rom. 15. 4–13 Luke 21. 25–33	Ps. 80 Baruch 5. 1–9 or Zeph. 3. 14–end Luke 1. 5–20	Ps. 40 (or 40. 12–end) 1 Kings 22. 1–28 2 Peter 3. 8–15a
Ps. *144*; 146 alt. Ps. 26; **28**; 29 Isa. 45. 14–end 1 Thess. ch. 1	P		Isa. 30. 1–18 Matt. 14. 1–12	Isa. 45. 14–end 1 Thess. ch. 1
Ps. **11**; 12; 13 alt. Ps. 33 Isa. ch. 46 1 Thess. 2. 1–12	P		Isa. 30. 19–end Matt. 14. 13–end	Isa. ch. 46 1 Thess. 2. 1–12
Ps. *10*; 14 alt. Ps. 119. 33–56 Isa. ch. 47 1 Thess. 2. 13–end	Pr	**Lucy, Martyr at Syracuse, 304** Com. Virgin Martyr	Isa. ch. 31 Matt. 15. 1–20	Isa. ch. 47 1 Thess. 2. 13–end
Ps. 73 alt. Ps. 39; **40** Isa. 48. 1–11 1 Thess. ch. 3	P		Isa. ch. 32 Matt. 15. 21–28	Isa. 48. 1–11 1 Thess. ch. 3

December 2017

			Sunday Principal Service / Weekday Eucharist	Third Service / Morning Prayer
15	F	Ember Day*		
			Isa. 48. 17–19	Ps. 85; *86*
			Ps. 1	*alt.* Ps. 31
			Matt. 11. 16–19	Isa. 33. 1–22
	P			Matt. 15. 29–end
16	Sa	Ember Day*		
			Ecclus. 48. 1–4, 9–11	Ps. 145
			or 2 Kings 2. 9–12	*alt.* Ps. 41; *42*; 43
			Ps. 80. 1–4, 18–19	Isa. ch. 35
			Matt. 17. 10–13	Matt. 16. 1–12
	P			
17	S	THE THIRD SUNDAY OF ADVENT		
		O Sapientia**		
			Isa. 61. 1–4, 8–end	Ps. 50. 1–6; 62
			Ps. 126	Isa. ch. 12
			or Canticle: Magnificat	Luke 1. 57–66
			1 Thess. 5. 16–24	
	P		John 1. 6–8, 19–28	
18	M		Jer. 23. 5–8	Ps. 40
			Ps. 72. 1–2, 12–13, 18–end	*alt.* Ps. 44
			Matt. 1. 18–24	Isa. 38. 1–8, 21–22
	P			Matt. 16. 13–end
19	Tu		Judg. 13. 2–7, 24–end	Ps. 144; *146*
			Ps. 71. 3–8	Isa. 38. 9–20
	P		Luke 1. 5–25	Matt. 17. 1–13
20	W		Isa. 7. 10–14	Ps. *46*; 95
			Ps. 24. 1–6	Isa. ch. 39
			Luke 1. 26–38	Matt. 17. 14–21
	P			
21	Th***		Zeph. 3. 14–18	Ps. *121*; 122; 123
			Ps. 33. 1–4, 11–12, 20–end	Zeph. 1.1 – 2.3
			Luke 1. 39–45	Matt. 17. 22–end
	P			
22	F		1 Sam. 1. 24–end	Ps. *124*; 125; 126; 127
			Ps. 113	Zeph. 3. 1–13
	P		Luke 1. 46–56	Matt. 18. 1–20
23	Sa		Mal. 3. 1–4; 4. 5–end	Ps. 128; 129; *130*; 131
			Ps. 25. 3–9	Zeph. 3. 14–end
	P		Luke 1. 57–66	Matt. 18. 21–end
24	S	THE FOURTH SUNDAY OF ADVENT		
		CHRISTMAS EVE	2 Sam. 7. 1–11, 16	Ps. 144
			Canticle: Magnificat	Isa. 7. 10–16
			or Ps. 89. 1–4, 19–26 (*or* 1–8)	Rom. 1. 1–7
			Rom. 16. 25–end	
			Luke 1. 26–38	
	P			

*For Ember Day provision, see p. 11.
**Evening Prayer readings from the Additional Weekday Lectionary (see p. 95) may be used from 17 to 23 December.
***Thomas the Apostle may be celebrated on 21 December instead of 3 July.

Second Service Evening Prayer	Calendar and Holy Communion	Morning Prayer	Evening Prayer
Ps. 82; **90** *alt.* Ps. 35 Isa. 48. 12–end 1 Thess. 4. 1–12 **P**		Isa. 33. 1–22 Matt. 15. 29–end	Isa. 48. 12–end 1 Thess. 4. 1–12
Ps. 93; **94** *alt.* Ps. 45; **46** Isa. 49. 1–13 1 Thess. 4. 13–end **ct**	O Sapientia **P**	Isa. ch. 35 Matt. 16. 1–12	Isa. 49. 1–13 1 Thess. 4. 13–end **ct**
Ps. 68. 1–19 (*or* 68. 1–8) Mal. 3. 1–4; ch. 4 Phil. 4. 4–7 *Gospel:* Matt. 14. 1–12	**THE THIRD SUNDAY IN ADVENT** Isa. ch. 35 Ps. 80. 1–7 1 Cor. 4. 1–5 Matt. 11. 2–10 **P**	Ps. 62 Isa. ch. 12 Luke 1. 57–66	Ps. 68. 1–19 (*or* 68. 1–8) Mal. 3. 1–4; ch. 4 Matt. 14. 1–12
Ps. 25; **26** *alt.* Ps. **47**; 49 Isa. 49. 14–25 1 Thess. 5. 1–11 **P**		Isa. 38. 1–8, 21–22 Matt. 16. 13–end	Isa. 49. 14–25 1 Thess. 5. 1–11
Ps. 10; **57** Isa. ch. 50 1 Thess. 5. 12–end **P**		Isa. 38. 9–20 Matt. 17. 1–13	Isa. ch. 50 1 Thess. 5. 12–end
Ps. **4**; 9 Isa. 51. 1–8 2 Thess. ch. 1	Ember Day Ember CEG **P**	Isa. ch. 39 Matt. 17. 14–21	Isa. 51. 1–8 2 Thess. ch. 1 *or First EP of Thomas the Apostle* (Ps. 27) Isa. ch. 35 Heb. 10.35 – 11.1 **R ct**
Ps. 80; **84** Isa. 51. 9–16 2 Thess. ch. 2	**THOMAS THE APOSTLE** Job 42. 1–6 Ps. 139. 1–11 Eph. 2. 19–end **R** John 20. 24–end	(Ps. 92; 146) 2 Sam. 15. 17–21 *or* Ecclus. ch. 2 John 11. 1–16	(Ps. 139) Hab. 2. 1–4 1 Pet. 1. 3–12
Ps. 24; **48** Isa. 51. 17–end 2 Thess. ch. 3	Ember Day Ember CEG **P**	Zeph. 3. 1–13 Matt. 18. 1–20	Isa. 51. 17–end 2 Thess. ch. 3
Ps. 89. 1–37 Isa. 52. 1–12 Jude **ct**	Ember Day Ember CEG **P**	Zeph. 3. 14–end Matt. 18. 21–end	Isa. 52. 1–12 Jude **ct**
Evening Prayer Ps. 85 Zech. ch. 2 Rev. 1. 1–8	**THE FOURTH SUNDAY IN ADVENT** **CHRISTMAS EVE** Collect (1) Christmas Eve (2) Advent 1 Isa. 40. 1–9 Ps. 145. 17–end Phil. 4. 4–7 **P** John 1. 19–28	Ps. 144 Isa. 7. 10–16 Rom. 1. 1–7	Ps. 85 Zech. ch. 2 Rev. 1. 1–8

December 2017

			Sunday Principal Service Weekday Eucharist	Third Service Morning Prayer
25	M	**CHRISTMAS DAY** *Any of the following sets of readings may* *be used on the evening of Christmas Eve* *and on Christmas Day. Set III should be* *used at some service during the* *celebration.*	I Isa. 9. 2–7 Ps. 96 Titus 2. 11–14 Luke 2. 1–14 [15–20] II Isa. 62. 6–end Ps. 97 Titus 3. 4–7 Luke 2. [1–7] 8–20 III Isa. 52. 7–10 Ps. 98 Heb. 1. 1–4 [5–12] John 1. 1–14	MP: Ps. *110*; 117 Isa. 62. 1–5 Matt. 1. 18–end
	⅏			
26	Tu	STEPHEN, DEACON, FIRST MARTYR	2 Chron. 24. 20–22 or Acts 7. 51–end Ps. 119. 161–168 Acts 7. 51–end or Gal. 2. 16b–20 Matt. 10. 17–22	MP: Ps. *13*; 31. 1–8; 150 Jer. 26. 12–15 Acts ch. 6
	R			
27	W	JOHN, APOSTLE AND EVANGELIST	Exod. 33. 7–11a Ps. 117 I John ch. 1 John 21. 19b–end	MP: Ps. *21*; 147. 13–end Exod. 33. 12–end I John 2. 1–11
	W			
28	Th	THE HOLY INNOCENTS	Jer. 31. 15–17 Ps. 124 I Cor. 1. 26–29 Matt. 2. 13–18	MP: Ps. *36*; 146 Baruch 4. 21–27 or Gen. 37. 13–20 Matt. 18. 1–10
	R			
29	F **Wr**	**Thomas Becket, Archbishop of Canterbury, Martyr, 1170*** Com. Martyr or *esp.* Matt. 10. 28–33 *also* Ecclus. 51. 1–8	I John 2. 3–11 Ps. 96. 1–4 Luke 2. 22–35	Ps. *19*; 20 Jonah ch. 1 Col. 1. 1–14
30	Sa W		I John 2. 12–17 Ps. 96. 7–10 Luke 2. 36–40	Ps. 111; 112; *113* Jonah ch. 2 Col. 1. 15–23
31	S W	THE FIRST SUNDAY OF CHRISTMAS	Isa. 61.10 – 62.3 Ps. 148 (or 148. 7–end) Gal. 4. 4–7 Luke 2. 15–21	Ps. 105. 1–11 Isa. 63. 7–9 Eph. 3. 5–12

*Thomas Becket may be celebrated on 7 July instead of 29 December.

Second Service Evening Prayer		Calendar and Holy Communion	Morning Prayer	Evening Prayer
		CHRISTMAS DAY		
EP: Ps. 8 Isa. 65. 17–25 Phil. 2. 5–11 or Luke 2. 1–20 if it has not been used at the principal service of the day		Isa. 9. 2–7 Ps. 98 Heb. 1. 1–12 John 1. 1–14	Ps. 110; 117 Isa. 62. 1–5 Matt. 1. 18–end	Ps. 8 Isa. 65. 17–25 Phil. 2. 5–11 or Luke 2. 1–20
	℘			
EP: Ps. 57; **86** Gen. 4. 1–10 Matt. 23. 34–end	R	STEPHEN, DEACON, FIRST MARTYR Collect (1) Stephen (2) Christmas 2 Chron. 24. 20–22 Ps. 119. 161–168 Acts 7. 55–end Matt. 23. 34–end	(Ps. 13; 31. 1–8; 150) Jer. 26. 12–15 Acts ch. 6	(Ps. 57; 86) Gen. 4. 1–10 Matt. 10. 17–22
EP: Ps. 97 Isa. 6. 1–8 1 John 5. 1–12	W	JOHN, APOSTLE AND EVANGELIST Collect (1) John (2) Christmas Exod. 33. 18–end Ps. 92. 11–end 1 John ch. 1 John 21. 19b–end	(Ps. 21; 147. 13–end) Exod. 33. 7–11a 1 John 2. 1–11	(Ps. 97) Isa. 6. 1–8 1 John 5. 1–12
EP: Ps. 123; **128** Isa. 49. 14–25 Mark 10. 13–16	R	THE HOLY INNOCENTS Collect (1) Innocents (2) Christmas Jer. 31. 10–17 Ps. 123 Rev. 14. 1–5 Matt. 2. 13–18	(Ps. 36; 146) Baruch 4. 21–27 or Gen. 37. 13–20 Matt. 18. 1–10	(Ps. 124; 128) Isa. 49. 14–25 Mark 10. 13–16
Ps. 131; **132** Isa. 57. 15–end John 1. 1–18	W	CEG of Christmas	Jonah ch. 1 Col. 1. 1–14	Isa. 57. 15–end John 1. 1–18
Ps. **65**; 84 Isa. 59. 1–15a John 1. 19–28 ct	W	CEG of Christmas	Jonah ch. 2 Col. 1. 15–23	Isa. 59. 1–15a John 1. 19–28 ct
Ps. 132 Isa. ch. 35 Col. 1. 9–20 or Luke 2. 41–end	W	THE SUNDAY AFTER CHRISTMAS DAY Isa. 62. 10–12 Ps. 45. 1–7 Gal. 4. 1–7 Matt. 1. 18–end	Ps. 105. 1–11 Isa. 63. 7–9 Eph. 3. 5–12	Ps. 132 Isa. ch. 35 1 John 1. 1–7

The *Common Worship* Additional Weekday Lectionary

The Additional Weekday Lectionary provides two readings on a one-year cycle for each day (except for Sundays, Principal Feasts and Holy Days, Festivals and Holy Week). They 'stand alone' and are intended particularly for use in those churches and cathedrals that attract occasional rather than regular congregations. The Additional Weekday Lectionary has been designed to complement rather than replace the existing Weekday Lectionary. Thus a church with a regular congregation in the morning and a congregation made up mainly of visitors in the evening would continue to use the Weekday Lectionary in the morning but might choose to use this Additional Weekday Lectionary for Evening Prayer.

Psalms are not provided, since the Weekday Lectionary already offers a variety of approaches with regard to psalmody. This Lectionary is not intended for use at the Eucharist; the Daily Eucharistic Lectionary is already authorized for that purpose.

On Sundays, Principal Feasts, other Principal Holy Days, Festivals, and in Holy Week, where no readings are provided in this table, the lectionary provision in the main part of this volume should be used.

Date		Old Testament	New Testament
November 2016			
27	S	THE FIRST SUNDAY OF ADVENT	
28	M	Mal. 3. 1–6	Matt. 3. 1–6
29	Tu	Zeph. 3. 14–end	I Thess. 4. 13–end
30	W	ANDREW	
December 2016			
I	Th	Mic. 5. 2–5a	John 3. 16–21
2	F	Isa. 66. 18–end	Luke 13. 22–30
3	Sa	Mic. 7. 8–15	Rom. 15.30 – 16.7, 25–end
4	S	THE SECOND SUNDAY OF ADVENT	
5	M	Jer. 7. 1–11	Phil. 4. 4–9
6	Tu	Dan. 7. 9–14	Matt. 24. 15–28
7	W	Amos 9. 11–end	Rom. 13. 8–14
8	Th	Jer. 23. 5–8	Mark 11. 1–11
9	F	Jer. 33. 14–22	Luke 21. 25–36
10	Sa	Zech. 14. 4–11	Rev. 22. 1–7
11	S	THE THIRD SUNDAY OF ADVENT	
12	M	Isa. 40. 1–11	Matt. 3. 1–12
13	Tu	Lam. 3. 22–33	I Cor. 1. 1–9
14	W	Joel 3. 9–16	Matt. 24. 29–35
15	Th	Isa. ch. 62	I Thess. 3. 6–13
16	F	Isa. 2. 1–5	Acts 11. 1–18
17	Sa	Ecclus. 24. 1–9 *or* Prov. 6. 22–31	I Cor. 2. 1–13
18	S	THE FOURTH SUNDAY OF ADVENT	
19	M	Isa. 11. 1–9	Rom. 15. 7–13
20	Tu	Isa. 22. 21–23	Rev. 3. 7–13
21	W	Num. 24. 15b–19	Rev. 22. 10–21
22	Th	Jer. 30. 7–11a	Acts 4. 1–12
23	F	Isa. 7. 10–15	Matt. 1. 18–23
24	Sa	*At Evening Prayer the readings for Christmas Eve are used. At other services, the following readings are used:*	
		Isa. 29. 13–18	I John 4. 7–16
25	S	**CHRISTMAS DAY**	
26	M	STEPHEN	
27	Tu	JOHN THE EVANGELIST	
28	W	THE HOLY INNOCENTS	
29	Th	Mic. 1. 1–4; 2. 12–13	Luke 2. 1–7
30	F	Isa. 9. 2–7	John 8. 12–20
31	Sa	Eccles. 3. 1–13	Rev. 21. 1–8
January 2017			
I	S	**NAMING AND CIRCUMCISION OF JESUS** (THE SECOND SUNDAY OF CHRISTMAS)	
2	M	Isa. 66. 6–14 *or Naming and Circumcision of Jesus*	Matt. 12. 46–50
3	Tu	Deut. 6. 4–15	John 10. 31–end
4	W	Isa. 63. 7–16	Gal. 3.23 – 4.7
5	Th	*At Evening prayer the readings for the Eve of Epiphany are used. At other services, or where, for pastoral reasons, The Epiphany is celebrated on Sunday 8 January, the following readings are used:*	
		Isa. ch. 12	2 Cor. 2. 12–end

Date		Old Testament	New Testament
6	F	**THE EPIPHANY**	
		Where, for pastoral reasons, The Epiphany is celebrated on Sunday 8 January, the following readings are used:	
		Gen. 25. 19–end	Eph. 1. 1–6
7	Sa	*Where The Baptism of Christ is celebrated on Sunday 8 January, the readings for the Eve of The Baptism of Christ are used at Evening Prayer. At other services, the following readings are used:*	
		Gen. 25. 19–end	Eph. 1. 1–6
		Where The Epiphany is celebrated on Sunday 8 January, the readings for the Eve of the Epiphany are used at Evening Prayer. At other services, the following readings are used:	
		Joel 2. 28–end	Eph. 1. 7–14
8	S	THE BAPTISM OF CHRIST (The First Sunday of Epiphany)	
9	M	*Where The Epiphany is celebrated on Friday 6 January and the Baptism of Christ on Sunday 8 January, these readings are used on Monday 9 January:*	
		Isa. 41. 14–20	John 1. 29–34
		Where The Epiphany is celebrated on Sunday 8 January, The Baptism of Christ is transferred to Monday 9 January.	
10	Tu	Exod. 17. 1–7	Acts 8. 26–end
11	W	Exod. 15. 1–19	Col. 2. 8–15
12	Th	Zech. 6. 9–15	I Pet. 2. 4–10
13	F	Isa. 51. 7–16	Gal. 6. 14–18
14	Sa	Lev. 16. 11–22	Heb. 10. 19–25
15	S	THE SECOND SUNDAY OF EPIPHANY	
16	M	I Kings. 17. 8–16	Mark 8. 1–10
17	Tu	I Kings 19. 1–9a	Mark 1. 9–15
18	W	I Kings 19. 9b–18	Mark 9. 2–13
19	Th	Lev. 11. 1–8, 13–19, 41–45	Acts 10. 9–16
20	F	Isa. 49. 8–13	Acts 10. 34–43
21	Sa	Gen. 35. 1–15	Acts 10. 44–end
22	S	THE THIRD SUNDAY OF EPIPHANY	
23	M	Ezek. 37. 15–end	John 17. 1–19
24	Tu	Ezek. 20. 39–44	John 17. 20–end
25	W	THE CONVERSION OF PAUL	
26	Th	Deut. 26. 16–end	Rom. 14. 1–9
27	F	Lev. 19. 9–28	Rom. 15. 1–7
28	Sa	Jer. 33. 1–11	I Pet. 5. 5b–end
		or, where The Presentation is celebrated on Sunday 29 January, First EP of Presentation of Christ	
29	S	THE FOURTH SUNDAY OF EPIPHANY (or The Presentation)	
30	M	Jonah ch. 3	2 Cor. 5. 11–21
31	Tu	Prov. 4. 10–end	Matt. 5. 13–20
February 2017			
I	W	Isa. 61. 1–9	Luke 7. 18–30
2	Th	**THE PRESENTATION** *or*	
		Isa. 52. 1–12	Matt. 10. 1–15
3	F	Isa. 56. 1–8	Matt. 28. 16–end
4	Sa	Hab. 2. 1–4	Rev. 14. 1–7
5	S	THE FOURTH SUNDAY BEFORE LENT	
6	M	Gen. 1. 26–end	Matt. 10. 1–16
7	Tu	Ruth 1. 1–18	I John 3. 14–end

Date		Old Testament	New Testament
8	W	1 Sam. 1. 19b–end	Luke 2. 41–end
9	Th	Gen. 47. 1–12	Eph. 3. 14–end
10	F	2 Sam. 1. 17–end	Rom. 8. 28–end
11	Sa	Song of Sol. 2. 8–end	1 Cor. ch. 13
12	S	THE THIRD SUNDAY BEFORE LENT	
13	M	Exod. 23. 1–13	James 2. 1–13
14	Tu	Deut. 10. 12–end	Heb. 13. 1–16
15	W	Isa. 58. 6–end	Matt. 25. 31–end
16	Th	Isa. 42. 1–9	Luke 4. 14–21
17	F	Amos 5. 6–15	Eph. 4. 25–end
18	Sa	Amos 5. 18–24	John 2. 13–22
19	S	THE SECOND SUNDAY BEFORE LENT	
20	M	Isa. 61. 1–9	Mark 6. 1–13
21	Tu	Isa. 52. 1–10	Rom. 10. 5–21
22	W	Isa. 52.13 – 53.6	Rom. 15. 14–21
23	Th	Isa. 53. 4–12	2 Cor. 4. 1–10
24	F	Zech. 8. 16–end	Matt. 10. 1–15
25	Sa	Jer. 1. 4–10	Matt. 10. 16–22
26	S	THE SUNDAY NEXT BEFORE LENT	
27	M	2 Kings 2. 13–22	3 John
28	Tu	Judg. 14. 5–17	Rev. 10. 4–11

March 2017

Date		Old Testament	New Testament
1	W	ASH WEDNESDAY	
2	Th	Gen. 2. 7–end	Heb. 2. 5–end
3	F	Gen. 4. 1–12	Heb. 4. 12–end
4	Sa	2 Kings 22. 11–end	Heb. 5. 1–10
5	S	THE FIRST SUNDAY OF LENT	
6	M	Gen. 6. 1–end; 7. 11–16	Luke 4. 14–21
7	Tu	Deut. 31. 7–13	1 John 3. 1–10
8	W	Gen. 11. 1–9	Matt. 24. 15–28
9	Th	Gen. 13. 1–13	1 Pet. 2. 13–end
10	F	Gen. 21. 1–8	Luke 9. 18–27
11	Sa	Gen. 32. 22–32	2 Pet. 1. 10–end
12	S	THE SECOND SUNDAY OF LENT	
13	M	1 Chron. 21. 1–17	1 John 2. 1–8
14	Tu	Zech. ch. 3	2 Pet. 2. 1–10a
15	W	Job. 1. 1–22	Luke 21.34 – 22.6
16	Th	2 Chron. 29. 1–11	Mark 11. 15–19
17	F	Exod. 19. 1–9a	1 Pet. 1. 1–9
18	Sa	Exod. 19. 9b–19	Acts 7. 44–50
19	S	THE THIRD SUNDAY OF LENT	
20	M	JOSEPH OF NAZARETH (transferred from 19th)	
21	Tu	Exod. 15. 22–27	Heb. 10. 32–end
22	W	Gen. 9. 8–17	1 Pet. 3. 18–end
23	Th	Dan. 12. 5–end	Mark 13. 21–end
24	F	Num. 20. 1–13	1 Cor. 10. 23–end
25	Sa	THE ANNUNCIATION	
26	S	THE FOURTH SUNDAY OF LENT (Mothering Sunday)	
27	M	2 Kings 24.18 – 25.7	1 Cor. 15. 20–34
28	Tu	Jer. 13. 12–19	Acts 13. 26–35
29	W	Jer. 13. 20–27	1 Pet. 1.17 – 2.3
30	Th	Jer. 22. 11–19	Luke 11. 37–52
31	F	Jer. 17. 1–14	Luke 6. 17–26

April 2017

Date		Old Testament	New Testament
1	Sa	Ezra ch. 1	2 Cor. 1. 12–19
2	S	THE FIFTH SUNDAY OF LENT (Passiontide begins)	
3	M	Joel 2. 12–17	2 John
4	Tu	Isa. 58. 1–14	Mark 10. 32–45
5	W	Joel 36. 1–12	John 14. 1–14
6	Th	Jer. 9. 17–22	Luke 13. 31–35
7	F	Lam. 5. 1–3, 19–22	John 12. 20–26
8	Sa	Job 17. 6–end	John 12. 27–36
9	S	PALM SUNDAY	
		HOLY WEEK	
16	S	EASTER DAY	
17	M	Isa. 54. 1–14	Rom. 1. 1–7

Date		Old Testament	New Testament
18	Tu	Isa. 51. 1–11	John 5. 19–29
19	W	Isa. 26. 1–19	John 20. 1–10
20	Th	Isa. 43. 14–21	Rev. 1. 4–end
21	F	Isa. 42. 10–17	1 Thess. 5. 1–11
22	Sa	Job 14. 1–14	John 21. 1–14
23	S	THE SECOND SUNDAY OF EASTER	
24	M	GEORGE (transferred from 23rd)	
25	Tu	MARK	
26	W	Hos. 5.15 – 6.6	1 Cor. 15. 1–11
27	Th	Jonah ch. 2	Mark 4. 35–end
28	F	Gen. 6. 9–end	1 Pet. 3. 8–end
29	Sa	1 Sam. 2. 1–8	Matt. 28. 8–15
30	S	THE THIRD SUNDAY OF EASTER	

May 2017

Date		Old Testament	New Testament
1	M	PHILIP AND JAMES	
2	Tu	Lev. 19. 9–18, 32–end	Matt. 5. 38–end
3	W	Gen. 3. 8–21	1 Cor. 15. 12–28
4	Th	Isa. 33. 13–22	Mark 6. 47–end
5	F	Neh. 9. 6–17	Rom. 5. 12–end
6	Sa	Isa. 61.10 – 62.5	Luke 24. 1–12
7	S	THE FOURTH SUNDAY OF EASTER	
8	M	Jer. 31. 10–17	Rev. 7. 9–end
9	Tu	Job 31. 13–23	Matt. 7. 1–12
10	W	Gen. 2. 4b–9	1 Cor. 15. 35–49
11	Th	Prov. 28. 3–end	Mark 10. 17–31
12	F	Eccles. 12. 1–8	Rom. 6. 1–11
13	Sa	1 Chron. 29. 10–13	Luke 24. 13–35
14	S	THE FIFTH SUNDAY OF EASTER	
15	M	MATTHIAS (transferred from 14th)	
		Where Matthias is celebrated on 24 February:	
		Gen. 15. 1–18	Rom. 4. 13–end
16	Tu	Deut. 8. 1–10	Matt. 6. 19–end
17	W	Hos. 13. 4–14	1 Cor. 15. 50–end
18	Th	Exod. 3. 1–15	Mark 12. 18–27
19	F	Ezek. 36. 33–end	Rom. 8. 1–11
20	Sa	Isa. 38. 9–20	Luke 24. 33–end
21	S	THE SIXTH SUNDAY OF EASTER	
22	M	Prov. 4. 1–13	Phil. 2. 1–11
23	Tu	Isa. 32. 12–end	Rom. 5. 1–11
24	W	*At Evening Prayer the readings for the Eve of Ascension Day are used. At other services, the following readings are used:*	
		Isa. 43. 1–13	Titus 2.11 – 3.8
25	Th	ASCENSION DAY	
26	F	Exod. 35.30 – 36.1	Gal. 5. 13–end
27	Sa	Num. 11. 16–17, 24–29	1 Cor. ch. 2
28	S	THE SEVENTH SUNDAY OF EASTER (Sunday after Ascension Day)	
29	M	Num. 27. 15–end	1 Cor. ch. 3
30	Tu	1 Sam. 10. 1–10	1 Cor. 12. 1–13
31	W	THE VISITATION	
		Where The Visitation is celebrated on 2 July:	
		1 Kings 19. 1–18	Matt. 3. 13–end

June 2017

Date		Old Testament	New Testament
1	Th	Ezek. 11. 14–20	Matt. 9.35 – 10.20
2	F	Ezek. 36. 22–28	Matt. 12. 22–32
3	Sa	*At Evening Prayer the readings for the Eve of Pentecost are used. At other services, the following readings are used:*	
		Mic. 3. 1–8	Eph. 6. 10–20
4	S	PENTECOST (Whit Sunday)	
5	M	Gen. 12. 1–9	Rom. 4. 13–end
6	Tu	Gen. 13. 1–12	Rom. 12. 9–end
7	W	Gen. ch. 15	Rom. 4. 1–8
8	Th	Gen. 22. 1–18	Heb. 11. 8–19
9	F	Isa. 51. 1–8	John 8. 48–end

Date		Old Testament	New Testament
10	Sa	*At Evening Prayer the readings for the Eve of Trinity Sunday are used. At other services, the following readings are used:*	
		Ecclus. 44. 19–23 or	James 2. 14–26
		Josh. 2. 1–15	
11	S	**TRINITY SUNDAY**	
12	M	**BARNABAS**	
13	Tu	Exod. 2. 11–end	Acts 7. 17–29
14	W	Exod. 3. 1–12	Acts 7. 30–38
15	Th	*Day of Thanksgiving for the Institution of Holy Communion (Corpus Christi), or, where Corpus Christi is celebrated as a Lesser Festival:*	
		Exod. 6. 1–13	John 9. 24–38
16	F	Exod. 34. 1–10	Mark 7. 1–13
17	Sa	Exod. 34. 27–end	2 Cor. 3. 7–end
18	S	**THE FIRST SUNDAY AFTER TRINITY**	
19	M	Gen. 37. 1–11	Rom. 11. 9–21
20	Tu	Gen. 41. 15–40	Mark 13. 1–13
21	W	Gen. 42. 17–end	Matt. 18. 1–14
22	Th	Gen. 45. 1–15	Acts 7. 9–16
23	F	Gen. 47. 1–12	1 Thess. 5. 12–end
24	Sa	**THE BIRTH OF JOHN THE BAPTIST**	
25	S	**THE SECOND SUNDAY AFTER TRINITY**	
26	M	Isa. ch. 32	James 3. 13–end
27	Tu	Prov. 3. 1–18	Matt. 5. 1–12
28	W	Judg. 6. 1–16	Matt. 5. 13–24
29	Th	**PETER AND PAUL**	
30	F	1 Sam. 16. 14–end	John 14. 15–end

July 2017

Date		Old Testament	New Testament
1	Sa	Isa. 6. 1–9	Rev. 19. 9–end
2	S	**THE THIRD SUNDAY AFTER TRINITY**	
3	M	**THOMAS**	
		Where Thomas is celebrated on 21 December:	
		Exod. 13. 13b–end	Luke 15. 1–10
4	Tu	Prov. 1. 20–end	James 5. 13–end
5	W	Isa. 5. 8–24	James 1. 17–25
6	Th	Isa. 57. 14–end	John 3. 1–17
7	F	Jer. 15. 15–end	Luke 16. 19–31
8	Sa	Isa. 25. 1–9	Acts 2. 22–33
9	S	**THE FOURTH SUNDAY AFTER TRINITY**	
10	M	Exod. 20. 1–17	Matt. 6. 1–15
11	Tu	Prov. 6. 6–19	Luke 4. 1–14
12	W	Isa. 24. 1–15	1 Cor. 6. 1–11
13	Th	Job ch. 7	Matt. 7. 21–29
14	F	Jer. 20. 7–end	Matt. 27. 27–44
15	Sa	Job ch. 28	Heb. 11.32 – 12.2
16	S	**THE FIFTH SUNDAY AFTER TRINITY**	
17	M	Exod. 32. 1–14	Col. 3. 1–11
18	Tu	Prov. 9. 1–12	2 Thess. 2.13 – 3.5
19	W	Isa. 26. 1–9	Rom. 8. 12–27
20	Th	Jer. 8.18 – 9.6	John 13. 21–35
21	F	2 Sam. 5. 1–12	Matt. 27. 45–56
22	Sa	**MARY MAGDALENE**	
23	S	**THE SIXTH SUNDAY AFTER TRINITY**	
24	M	Exod. 40. 1–16	Luke 14. 15–24
25	Tu	**JAMES**	
26	W	Isa. 33. 2–10	Phil. 1. 1–11
27	Th	Job ch. 38	Luke 18. 1–14
28	F	Job 42. 1–6	John 3. 1–15
29	Sa	Eccles. 9. 1–11	Heb. 1. 1–9
30	S	**THE SEVENTH SUNDAY AFTER TRINITY**	
31	M	Num. 23. 1–12	1 Cor. 1. 10–17

August 2017

Date		Old Testament	New Testament
1	Tu	Prov. 12. 1–12	Gal. 3. 1–14
2	W	Isa. 49. 8–13	2 Cor. 8. 1–11
3	Th	Hos. ch. 14	John 15. 1–17

Date		Old Testament	New Testament
4	F	2 Sam. 18. 18–end	Matt. 27. 57–66
5	Sa	Isa. 55. 1–7	Mark 6. 1–8
6	S	**THE TRANSFIGURATION (THE EIGHTH SUNDAY AFTER TRINITY)**	
7	M	*Where the Transfiguration is celebrated on Sunday 6 August:*	
		Joel 3. 16–21	Mark 4. 21–34
8	Tu	Prov. 12. 13–end	John 1. 43–51
9	W	Isa. 55. 8–end	2 Tim. 2. 8–19
10	Th	Isa. 38. 1–8	Mark 5. 21–43
11	F	Jer. 14. 1–9	Luke 8. 4–15
12	Sa	Eccles. 5. 10–19	1 Tim. 6. 6–16
13	S	**THE NINTH SUNDAY AFTER TRINITY**	
14	M	Josh. 1. 1–9	1 Cor. 9. 19–end
15	Tu	**THE BLESSED VIRGIN MARY**	
		Where the Blessed Virgin Mary is celebrated on 8 September:	
		Prov. 15. 1–11	Gal. 2. 15–end
16	W	Isa. 49. 1–7	1 John ch. 1
17	Th	Prov. 27. 1–12	John 15. 12–27
18	F	Isa. 59. 8–end	Mark 15. 6–20
19	Sa	Zech. 7.8 – 8.8	Luke 20. 27–40
20	S	**THE TENTH SUNDAY AFTER TRINITY**	
21	M	Judg. 13. 1–23	Luke 10. 38–42
22	Tu	Prov. 15. 15–end	Matt. 15. 21–28
23	W	Isa. 45. 1–7	Eph. 4. 1–16
24	Th	**BARTHOLOMEW**	
25	F	Jer. 18. 1–11	Heb. 1. 1–9
26	Sa	Jer. 26. 1–19	Eph. 3. 1–13
27	S	**THE ELEVENTH SUNDAY AFTER TRINITY**	
28	M	Ruth 2. 1–13	Luke 10. 25–37
29	Tu	Prov. 16. 1–11	Phil. 3. 4b–end
30	W	Deut. 11. 1–21	2 Cor. 9. 6–end
31	Th	Ecclus. ch. 2 or	John 16. 1–15
		Eccles. 2. 12–25	

September 2017

Date		Old Testament	New Testament
1	F	Obad. 1–10	John 19. 1–16
2	Sa	2 Kings 2. 11–14	Luke 24. 36–end
3	S	**THE TWELFTH SUNDAY AFTER TRINITY**	
4	M	1 Sam. 17. 32–50	Matt. 8. 14–22
5	Tu	Prov. 17. 1–15	Luke 7. 1–17
6	W	Jer. 5. 20–end	2 Pet. 3. 8–end
7	Th	Dan. 2. 1–23	Luke 10. 1–20
8	F	Dan. 3. 1–28	Rev. ch. 15
9	Sa	Dan. ch. 6	Phil. 2. 14–24
10	S	**THE THIRTEENTH SUNDAY AFTER TRINITY**	
11	M	2 Sam. 7. 4–17	2 Cor. 5. 1–10
12	Tu	Prov. 18. 10–21	Rom. 14. 10–end
13	W	Judg. 4. 1–10	Rom. 1. 8–17
14	Th	**HOLY CROSS DAY**	
15	F	Job 1. 1–24	Mark 15. 21–32
16	Sa	Exod. 19. 1–9	John 20. 11–18
17	S	**THE FOURTEENTH SUNDAY AFTER TRINITY**	
18	M	Hag. ch. 1	Mark 7. 9–23
19	Tu	Prov. 21. 1–18	Mark 6. 30–44
20	W	Hos. 11. 1–11	1 John 4. 9–end
21	Th	**MATTHEW**	
22	F	2 Kings 19. 4–18	1 Thess. ch. 3
23	Sa	Ecclus. 4. 11–28 or	2 Tim. 3. 10–end
		Deut. 29. 2–15	
24	S	**THE FIFTEENTH SUNDAY AFTER TRINITY**	
25	M	Wisd. 6. 12–21 or	Matt. 15. 1–9
		Job 12. 1–16	
26	Tu	Prov. 8. 1–11	Luke 6. 39–end
27	W	Prov. 2. 1–15	Col. 1. 9–20
28	Th	Baruch 3. 14–end or	John 1. 1–18
		Gen. 1. 1–13	

Date		Old Testament	New Testament
29	F	MICHAEL AND ALL ANGELS	
30	Sa	Wisd. 9. 1–12 or Jer. 1. 4–10	Luke 2. 41–end

October 2017

Date		Old Testament	New Testament
1	S	THE SIXTEENTH SUNDAY AFTER TRINITY	
2	M	Gen. 21. 1–13	Luke 1. 26–38
3	Tu	Ruth 4. 7–17	Luke 2. 25–38
4	W	2 Kings 4. 1–7	John 2. 1–11
5	Th	2 Kings 4. 25b–37	Mark 3. 19b–35
6	F	Judith 8. 9–17, 28–36 or Ruth 1. 1–18	John 19. 25b–30
7	Sa	Exod. 15. 19–27	Acts 1. 6–14
8	S	THE SEVENTEENTH SUNDAY AFTER TRINITY	
9	M	Exod. 19. 16–end	Heb. 12. 18–end
10	Tu	1 Chron. 16. 1–13	Rev. 11. 15–end
11	W	1 Chron. 29. 10–19	Col. 3. 12–17
12	Th	Neh. 8. 1–12	1 Cor. 14. 1–12
13	F	Isa. 1. 10–17	Mark 12. 28–34
14	Sa	Dan. 6. 6–23	Rev. 12. 7–12
15	S	THE EIGHTEENTH SUNDAY AFTER TRINITY	
16	M	2 Sam. 22. 4–7, 17–20	Heb. 7.26 – 8.6
17	Tu	Prov. 22. 17–end	2 Cor. 12. 1–10
18	W	LUKE	
19	Th	Isa. 24. 1–15	John 16. 25–33
20	F	Jer. 14. 1–9	Luke 23. 44–56
21	Sa	Zech. 8. 14–end	John 20. 19–end
22	S	THE NINETEENTH SUNDAY AFTER TRINITY	
23	M	1 Kings 3. 3–14	1 Tim. 3.13 – 4.8
24	Tu	Prov. 27. 11–end	Gal. 6. 1–10
25	W	Isa. 51. 1–6	2 Cor. 1. 1–11
26	Th	Ecclus. 18. 1–14 or Job ch. 26	1 Cor. 11. 17–end
27	F	Ecclus. 28. 2–12 or Job 19. 21–end	Mark 15. 33–37
28	Sa	SIMON AND JUDE	
29	S	THE LAST SUNDAY AFTER TRINITY	
30	M	Isa. 42. 14–21	Luke 1. 5–25
31	Tu	At Evening Prayer the readings for the Eve of All Saints are used. At other services, the following readings are used:	
		1 Sam. 4. 12–end	Luke 1. 57–80

November 2017

Date		Old Testament	New Testament
1	W	**ALL SAINTS' DAY**	
		or, where All Saints' Day is celebrated on Sunday 5 November:	
		Baruch ch. 5 or Hag. 1. 1–11	Mark 1. 1–11
2	Th	Isa. ch. 35	Matt. 11. 2–19
3	F	2 Sam. 11. 1–17	Matt. 14. 1–12
4	Sa	Isa. 43. 15–21	Acts 19. 1–10
5	S	THE FOURTH SUNDAY BEFORE ADVENT	
6	M	Esther 3. 1–11; 4. 7–17	Matt. 18. 1–10
7	Tu	Ezek. 18. 21–end	Matt. 18. 12–20
8	W	Prov. 3. 27–end	Matt. 18. 21–end
9	Th	Exod. 23. 1–9	Matt. 19. 1–15
10	F	Prov. 3. 13–18	Matt. 19. 16–end
11	Sa	Deut. 28. 1–6	Matt. 20. 1–16
12	S	THE THIRD SUNDAY BEFORE ADVENT	
13	M	Isa. 40. 21–end	Rom. 11. 25–end
14	Tu	Ezek. 34. 20–end	John 10. 1–18
15	W	Lev. 26. 3–13	Titus 2. 1–10
16	Th	Hos. 6. 1–6	Matt. 9. 9–13
17	F	Mal. ch. 4	John 4. 5–26
18	Sa	Mic. 6. 6–8	Col. 3. 12–17
19	S	THE SECOND SUNDAY BEFORE ADVENT	
20	M	Mic. 7. 1–7	Matt. 10. 24–39
21	Tu	Hab. 3. 1–19a	1 Cor. 4. 9–16
22	W	Zech. 8. 1–13	Mark 13. 3–8
23	Th	Zech. 10. 6–end	1 Pet. 5. 1–11
24	F	Mic. 4. 1–5	Luke 9. 28–36
25	Sa	At Evening Prayer the readings for the Eve of Christ the King are used. At other services, the following readings are used:	
		Exod. 16. 1–21	John 6. 3–15
26	S	CHRIST THE KING (The Sunday next before Advent)	
27	M	Jer. 30. 1–3, 10–17	Rom. 12. 9–21
28	Tu	Jer. 30. 18–24	John 10. 22–30
29	W	Jer. 31. 1–9	Matt. 15. 21–31
30	Th	ANDREW	

December 2017

Date		Old Testament	New Testament
1	F	Jer. 31. 31–37	Heb. 10. 11–18
2	Sa	Isa. 51.17 – 52.2	Eph. 5. 1–20
3	S	THE FIRST SUNDAY OF ADVENT	
4	M	Mal. 3. 1–6	Matt. 3. 1–6
5	Tu	Zeph. 3. 14–end	1 Thess. 4. 13–end
6	W	Isa. 65.17 – 66.2	Matt. 24. 1–14
7	Th	Mic. 5. 2–5a	John 3. 16–21
8	F	Isa. 66. 18–end	Luke 13. 22–30
9	Sa	Mic. 7. 8–15	Rom. 15.30 – 16.7, 25–end
10	S	THE SECOND SUNDAY OF ADVENT	
11	M	Jer. 7. 1–11	Phil. 4. 4–9
12	Tu	Dan. 7. 9–14	Matt. 24. 15–28
13	W	Amos 9. 11–end	Rom. 13. 8–14
14	Th	Jer. 23. 5–8	Mark 11. 1–11
15	F	Jer. 33. 14–22	Luke 21. 25–36
16	Sa	Zech. 14. 4–11	Rev. 22. 1–7
17	S	THE THIRD SUNDAY OF ADVENT	
18	M	Exod. 3. 1–6	Acts 7. 20–36
19	Tu	Isa. 11. 1–9	Rom. 15. 7–13
20	W	Isa. 22. 21–23	Rev. 3. 7–13
21	Th	Num. 24. 15b–19	Rev. 22. 10–21
22	F	Jer. 30. 7–11a	Acts 4. 1–12
23	Sa	Isa. 7. 10–15	Matt. 1. 18–23
24	S	THE FOURTH SUNDAY OF ADVENT (Christmas Eve)	
25	M	**CHRISTMAS DAY**	
26	Tu	STEPHEN	
27	W	JOHN THE EVANGELIST	
28	Th	THE HOLY INNOCENTS	
29	F	Mic. 1. 1–4; 2. 12–13	Luke 2. 1–7
30	Sa	Isa. 9. 2–7	John 8. 12–20
31	S	THE FIRST SUNDAY OF CHRISTMAS	

CALENDAR 2017

JANUARY · FEBRUARY · MARCH
APRIL · MAY · JUNE
JULY · AUGUST · SEPTEMBER
OCTOBER · NOVEMBER · DECEMBER

CALENDAR 2018

JANUARY · FEBRUARY · MARCH
APRIL · MAY · JUNE
JULY · AUGUST · SEPTEMBER
OCTOBER · NOVEMBER · DECEMBER

A = Ash Wednesday, Ascension, Advent
A⁻ = Before Advent
A⁻⁴ = also All Saints, 2017 and 2018 (if trans.)

A⁻¹ = Christ the King
An = Annunciation
AS = All Saints
B = Baptism
E = Epiphany, Easter

E⁴ = also Presentation, 2017 and 2018 (if trans.)
G = Good Friday
L = Lent

L⁻ = Before Lent
M = Maundy Thursday
P = Palm Sunday
Pr = Presentation
T = Trinity

T⁻¹ = Last Sunday after Trinity
W = Pentecost (Whit Sunday)
X = Christmas

(T⁴ = also Birth of John the Baptist, 2018)
(T⁸ = also Transfiguration, 2017; also Mary Magdalene, 2018)

In 2017, The Baptism of Christ or The Epiphany may be celebrated on Sunday 8 January. Where The Epiphany is celebrated on the Sunday, The Baptism is transferred to Monday 9 January.
In 2018, The Baptism of Christ or The Epiphany may be celebrated on Sunday 7 January. Where The Epiphany is celebrated on the Sunday, The Baptism is transferred to Monday 8 January.